The Laboratory Cockroach

The Laboratory Cockroach

Experiments in cockroach anatomy, physiology and behavior

William J. Bell
University of Kansas
Lawrence, Kansas

London   New York
CHAPMAN AND HALL

First published 1981
by Chapman and Hall Ltd
11 New Fetter Lane, London EC4P 4EE

Published in the USA by
Chapman and Hall
in association with Methuen, Inc.
733 Third Avenue, New York, NY10017

© 1981 W. J. Bell

Printed in Great Britain by
J. W. Arrowsmith Ltd, Bristol

ISBN 0 412 23990 6

British Library Cataloguing in Publication Data

Bell, William J.
   The laboratory cockroach.
   1. Cockroaches—Laboratory manuals
   I. Title
   595.7'22   QL505.5

   ISBN 0-412-23990-6

TABLE OF CONTENTS

PREFACE

Cockroaches are ideal subjects for laboratory investigation at all educational levels. Compared with many other laboratory animals, cockroaches are easily and inexpensively maintained and cultured and require relatively little space. They are hardy and are readily available.

The purpose of this book is to provide background material and experimental leads for utilizing cockroaches in the teaching laboratory and in designing research projects. The level of difficulty of the experiments varies according to the depth of understanding desired by the instructor. In most cases at least a part of each experiment or technique can be incorporated into the laboratory component of elementary, high school or college curriculum. Sections of the lab book are appropriate for courses in Animal Behavior, Entomology, Organismic Biology and Insect Physiology. Aside from this main purpose, the book also provides a wealth of experimental ideas and techniques for a scientist at any level of education.

Lawrence, Kansas
June 15, 1981

W.J.B.

ACKNOWLEDGEMENTS.   Virtually all graduate students who have worked on cockroach research in my laboratory have knowingly or unknowingly contributed to this book.   The most important contribution was from Sandy Jones McPeak, who encouraged me to finish the project.   Segments of various chapters were conceived, developed or reviewed by Michael D. Breed, Sandy Jones McPeak, Michael K. Rust, Coby Schal, Thomas R. Tobin, W. Alexander Hawkins, Gary R. Sams and Chris Parsons Sams. I am most grateful to authors and publishing companies for allowing me to reproduce their published illustrative materials; these sources are listed in an appropriate section of the book.   I am indebted to Coletta Spencer, Jan Elder and Tammi Harbert for their patience and artistry in preparing the manuscript, to Sharon Hagan for explaining how to prepare a manuscript for photocopy processing, and to Mary McCoy for original illustrations.   High contrast cockroach photographs on the cover and on topic heading pages were skillfully prepared by my colleague, Michael K. Tourtellot. Professors D.M. Guthrie and George W. Byers kindly read and criticized portions of an earlier draft.

-- W. J. B.

Topic——**1**——COCKROACH DIVERSITY AND IDENTIFICATION

There are more than 4,000 known species of cockroaches throughout the world, most of which live in the tropics. Aside from living in our houses, cockroaches inhabit leaf litter and tree bark in temperate and tropical forests, grasslands, desert sand dunes, rotting logs, bird and ant nests, and caves. Cockroaches, being primitive insects, are relatives of termites (order Isoptera) and grasshoppers, crickets and katydids (order Orthoptera). The presently accepted scheme of classification places cockroaches in the order Dictyoptera and suborder Blattaria. The other suborder, Mantodea, contains the preying mandids. There are five major families of cockroaches: Cryptocercidae, Blattidae, Blaberidae, Blattellidae and Polyphagidae.

A. IDENTIFICATION. There are various ways to identify cockroaches, using external morphological characteristics, body size and shape of the ootheca (egg case). Information for identification is provided here in three ways: (1) photographs of cockroach species, (2) descriptions in Table I, and (3) a key to common cockroaches. It is probably wise to study and complete Exercise 4.1 on external anatomy before attempting to identify cockroaches with the key.

B. THREE PRINCIPAL SPECIES. The three most common cockroach species in North America and Europe are the American cockroach, Periplaneta americana (family Blattidae), Oriental cockroach, Blatta orientalis (family Blattidae), and German cockroach, Blattella germanica (family Blattellidae). Depending on your geographical location either of the first two might be called 'water bugs.' Since all three species originated in Africa, the references to origin are less than meaningful.

Periplaneta americana is the largest common cockroach species. (Fig. 1.1). It is especially common in urban areas and in southern parts of the U.S. Both sexes have fully developed wings, and males occasionally fly or glide. Identifiers: reddish-brown, large body (29 - 44 mm), yellow blotch on pronotum. Three closely related species, P. brunnea, P. australasiae and P. fuliginosa look similar to P. americana and are found in sub-tropical regions throughout much of the world.

Blattella germanica is the smallest pest species (Fig. 1.2). Both sexes are winged. The German cockroach is now found in all areas of the U.S. and Europe, and is considered to be the most important pest cockroach. Identifiers: small (10 - 15 mm), tan appearance.

Blatta orientalis commonly occurs in sewers, basements and other 'below-ground-level' structures. Females are wingless; males have short wings (Fig. 1.3). Identifiers: shiny black appearance, stout bodies (18 - 27 mm).

C. OTHER COMMON SPECIES. Supella longipalpa (family Blattellidae) (Fig. 1.4), the 'brown-banded cockroach,' is quickly spreading throughout the world as a pest species. It can survive in relatively dry habitats, feeding on book bindings and other types of glue. Identifiers: slender, small (10 - 15 mm), light tan appearance; adults have wings; nymphs have brown bands on thorax and abdomen.

Parcoblatta pennsylvanica (family Blattellidae) is a common cockroach in woodlands throughout the U.S. (Fig. 1.5). Males fly to lights at night,

1

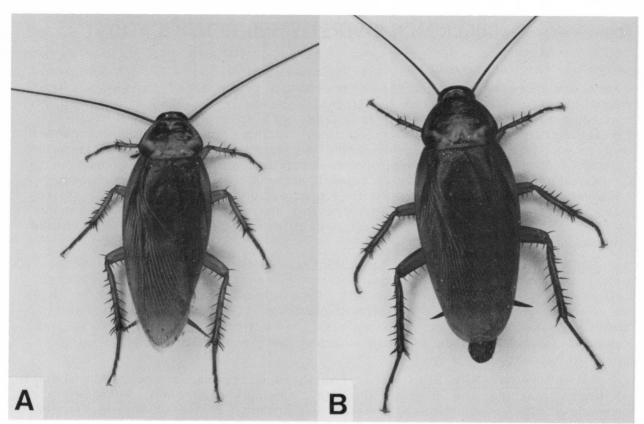

Fig. 1.1. American cockroach, <u>Periplaneta</u> <u>americana</u>; (A) male (B) female.

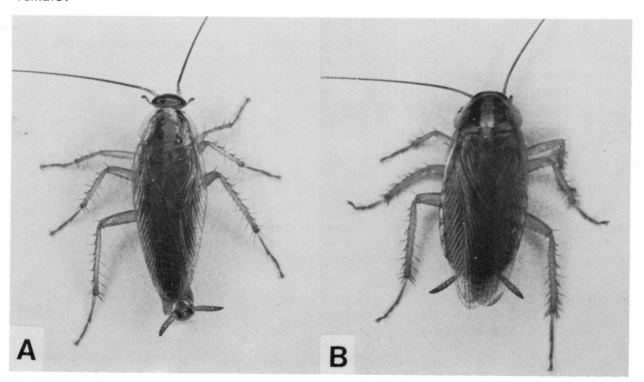

Fig. 1.2. German cockroach, <u>Blattella</u> <u>germanica</u>; (A) male (B) female.

and nymphs are often found under outdoor piles of firewood or rotting logs. Identifiers: males and females dark brown, (13 - 30 mm), thorax and forewings edged with white or yellow. Other species of this genus also are fairly common (Parcoblatta bolliana, P. fulvescens, P. lata, P. uhleriana, and P. virginica). The European counterpart of Parcoblatta is Ectobius, a small wood cockroach. Recently Ectobius has also appeared in New England.

Eurycotis floridana (family Blattidae) is a large cockroach often observed outdoors in Florida and in the West Indies (Fig. 1.6). Identifiers: adults wingless, large (30 - 40 mm), red-brown to black; nymphs with yellow stripes. Adults secrete a defensive odor that smells of almonds.

Cryptocercus punctulatus (family Cryptocercidae) is a social cockroach, living in family groups within rotting logs. It is found only in oak-hickory forests in the Appalachians and in the far northwestern U.S. Identifiers: adults large, (23 - 30 mm) and wingless; homogeneous dark-brown; pronotum is thick and grooved; eyes very small; cerci very small (the name Cryptocercus implies 'hidden cerci').

D. TROPICAL SPECIES. The following species are found in tropical, and sometimes, subtropical regions. A few are pests. Colonies of these species are maintained by entomologists who study cockroach biology.

Several species of Gromphadorhina (family Blaberidae) live only in Madagascar, the island off the east coast of Africa. Some species are very large (up to 65 mm). Adults 'hiss' when disturbed and employ the hissing sounds in aggressive and sexual behavior.

Blaberus (family Blaberidae) is a common tropical genus, including Blaberus craniifer (48 - 57 mm) (Fig. 1.7), which is established in Florida and Blaberus giganteus (70 - 80 mm), which is found mainly in tropical rainforests. Males and females are good fliers, often appearing at swimming pools or hotel patios at night.

Two species that are common in tropical regions, Nauphoeta cinerea (25 - 29 mm) and Leucophaea maderae (40 - 50 mm) (family Blaberidae), have now been found in the U.S. L. Maderae (Fig. 1.8) is well established indoors in New York City.

E. CHARACTERISTICS OF COCKROACHES. Table I summarizes a lot of information about cockroaches that might be of value in identifying species and planning experiments. 'Reproduction characteristics' refers to the disposition of the egg cases during egg development; oviparous means that the egg case is held outside the body, ovoviviparous means that it is held inside the body. 'Nymph development' relates the time from when nymphs hatch from an eggcase to when they reach adulthood.

F. KEY TO ADULTS OF COMMON COCKROACHES. To use the key beginning on page 10, follow in sequence beginning with couplet number 1. Refer to the figures as required. The external anatomy exercise (4.1) should be completed before attempting to use the key.

G. SOURCES OF INFORMATION ABOUT COCKROACHES. Four excellent books are available on cockroaches: The Biology of the Cockroach (1968) by D. M. Guthrie and A. R. Tindall, Edward Arnold Ltd., 41 Maddox St., London W1, 408 pp.; The Cockroach, Vol. I (1968) by P. B. Cornwell, Rentokil Library, Hutchinson Press, 178-202 Great Portland St., London

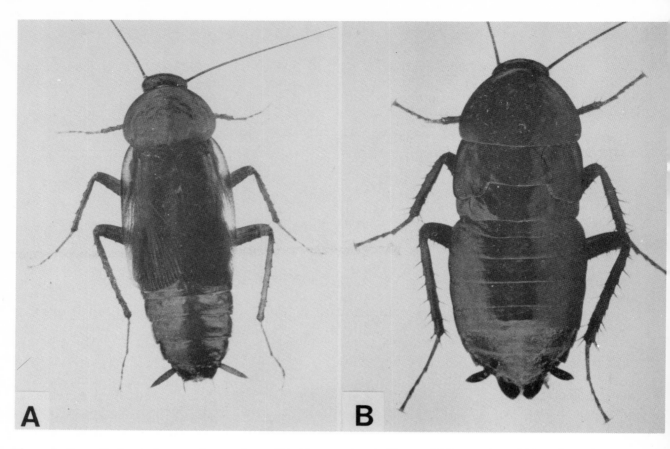

Fig. 1.3. Oriental cockroach, _Blatta orientalis_; (A) male (B) female.

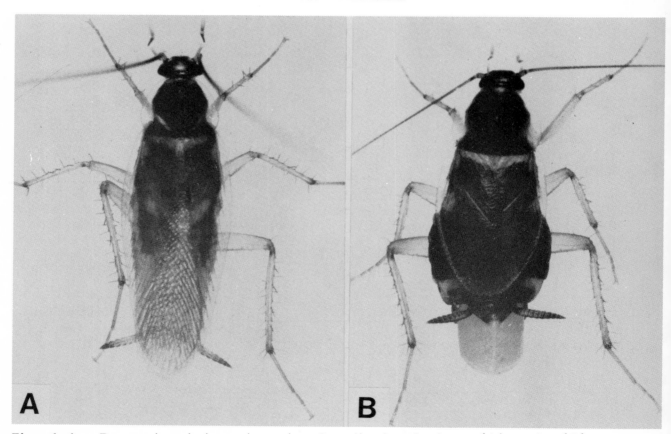

Fig. 1.4. Brown-banded cockroach, _Supella longipalpa_; (A) male (B) female.

4

W1, 391 pp.; The Cockroach, Vol II (1976), by P. B. Cornwell (same publisher as above); The American Cockroach (1981), edited by W. J. Bell and K. G. Adiyodi, Chapman & Hall, London, 550 pp.

Except for Cornwell's Vol. II, which mainly concerns cockroach control, the books cover the following topics: exoskeleton, reproduction, metamorphosis, hormones, nervous system, behavior, muscles and locomotion, feeding and digestion, metabolism, excretion, circulation, respiration and natural history. At least one of these books should be available as a resource for students experimenting with cockroaches.

References are provided at the end of each chapter for readings in the general subject area (GENERAL READINGS) and for more details and technical information (RESEARCH REPORTS). In some chapters, as noted, the readings are essential either for carrying out the experiments (where the techniques are very complicated) or for a complete understanding of the concepts involved.

GENERAL READINGS

Cameron, E. 1961. The cockroach, Periplaneta americana L. London: Heinemann.

Cornwell, P. B. 1968. Chapters 2 and 3. In: The Cockroach. London: Hutchinson Press.

McKittrick, F. A. 1964. Evolutionary Studies of Cockroaches. Memoir 389, Cornell Univ. Agric. Expt. Sta.

Roth, L. M. 1981. Introduction to Periplaneta. In: The American Cockroach. Ed. by W. J. Bell and K. G. Adiyodi. London: Chapman & Hall.

Roth L. M. and E. R. Willis. 1960. The biotic associations of cockroaches. Smithsonian Misc. Collect. 141: 1-470.

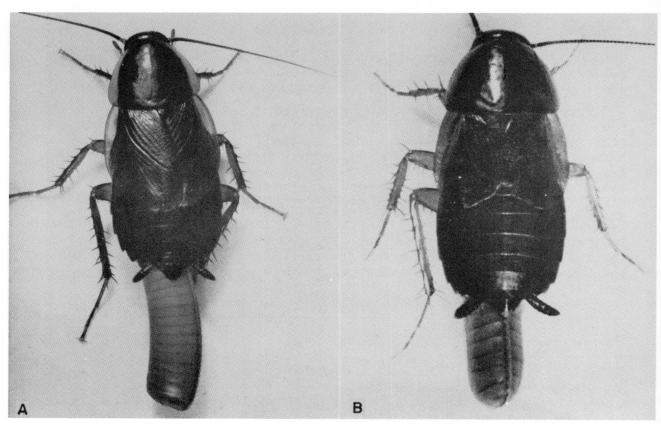

Fig. 1.5. Wood cockroaches; (A) female <u>Parcoblatta</u> <u>pennsylvanica</u> (B) female <u>Parcoblatta</u> <u>virginica</u>.

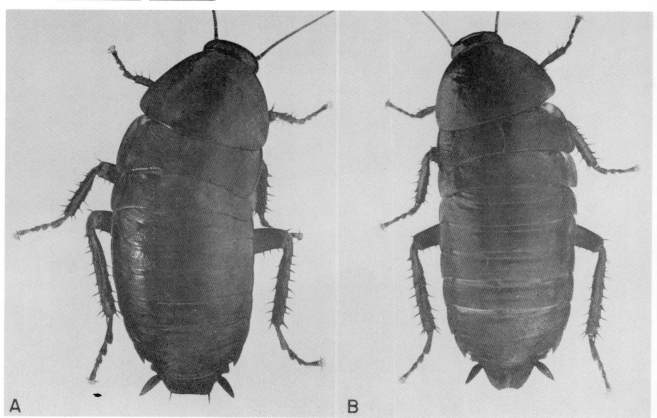

Fig. 1.6. <u>Eurycotis</u> <u>floridana</u>; (A) male (B) female.

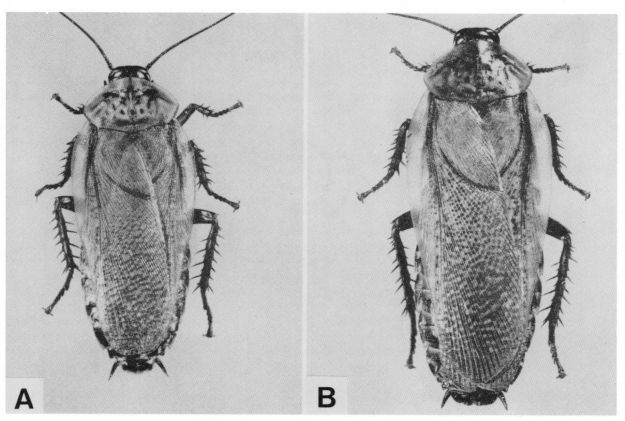

Fig. 1.8. _Leucophaea maderae_; (A) male (B) female.

Fig. 1.7. _Blaberus craniifer_; (A) male (B) female.

TABLE 1. Characteristics of cockroaches

Scientific name and common name	Morphological Characteristics	Body Length (mm) Male	Female	Egg case; Reproduction Characteristics	Nymph development	Interval between egg cases	Habitat	Geographical distribution
Periplaneta americana American cockroach	Reddish-brown; full wings	36-44	29-37	8x5 mm, dark brown; Oviparous	6-12 mo.	5-6 days	Domiciliary, caves, outdoors	World-wide (temperate, subtropical, tropical)
Blatta orientalis Oriental cockroach	Black to very dark brown; females wingless, males reduced wings	17-29	20-27	10x5 mm, dark brown to black; Oviparous	5-7 mo.	6-8 days	Domiciliary	World-wide (temperate, subtropical, tropical)
Blattella germanica German cockroach	Tan or pale yellowish brown; full wings	10-13	12-15	8x3 mm, tan; Oviparous	36-63 days	22 days	Domiciliary	World-wide (temperate, subtropical, tropical)
Supella longipalpa Brown-banded cockroach	Tan and brown; lighter margins on pronotum, wings; full wings	13-15	10-12	4x2.5 mm, reddish-brown; Oviparous	54-100 days; nymphs with light bands	6 days?	Domiciliary	World-wide (temperate, subtropical, tropical)
Periplaneta australasiae Australian cockroach	Reddish-brown; yellowish wing margins; dark pronotum surrounded by by yellow edges; full wings	36-44	29-37	10x5 mm, dark brown; Oviparous	6-12 mo; nymphs with yellow bands	10 days	Outdoors; some-times domiciliary	World-wide (subtropical, tropical)
Periplaneta brunnea brown cockroach	Reddish-brown; dark pronotum surrounded by tan edges; full wings	34-42	27-35	12-16 mm, reddish-brown, securely glued to substrate; Oviparous		4 days	Outdoors; some-times domiciliary	World-wide (temperate, subtropical)
Periplaneta fuliginosa smoky brown cockroach	Brownish black	36-44	29-37	10-13 mm; Oviparous	179-586 days	11 days	Outdoors; some-times domiciliary	World-wide (subtropical)
Pycnoscelus surinamensis surinam cockroach	Brownish black; light wing margins; full wings	18-24		Ovoviviparous	127-184 days		Outdoors, greenhouses	World-wide (subtropical, tropical)
Leucophaea maderae Madeira cockroach	Olive; full wings mottled with dark lines	40-44	42-50	Ovoviviparous	127-150 days		Domiciliary, agricultural products; warehouses	World-wide (subtropical, tropical)

Scientific name and common name	Morphological Characteristics	Body Length (mm) Male	Female	Egg case; Reproduction Characteristics	Nymph development	Interval between egg cases	Habitat	Geographical distribution
Nauphoeta cinerea Lobster cockroach	Ash colored with blotchy pattern on pronotum; wings shorter than abdomen	25-29		Ovoviviparous	72-94 days		Outdoors; sometimes domiciliary	World-wide (subtropical, tropical)
Blaberus craniifer	Blackish brown, pronotum elliptical and ornamented with design in center; full wings	48-50	54-57	Ovoviviparous			Outdoors, sometime domiciliary	Central and S. America West Indies (subtropical, tropical)
Eurycotis floridana	Reddish brown to black; wingless	31-35	30-40	14-16 mm, black; Oviparous	100 days; nymphs with yellow bands		Outdoors, shelters, stumps	Central and S. America, West Indies (subtropical, tropical)
Parcoblatta sp. Wood roaches (5 species)	Yellowish brown to black			Oviparous			Woodlands, grasslands	U.S. (temperate)
Cryptocercus punctulatus	Homogeneous black; wingless			Oviparous			Woodlands	U.S. (temperate)
Ectobius sp. (3 species)	Yellowish brown to brown	6-11		Oviparous			Woodlands, grasslands	Europe (temperate)
Arenivaga sp. Desert cockroach	Light tan			Oviparous			Desert	U.S. (temperate)
Blattella vaga Field cockroach	Tan; longitudinal dark band on pronotum; full wings	9-10	8-10	Oviparous	45-90 days	24 days	Sometimes domiciliary, grasslands, desert	World wide (temperate, subtropical)

KEY TO THE ADULTS OF COCKROACHES WHICH MOST COMMONLY BREED IN, OR MAY OCCASIONALLY BE FOUND IN BUILDINGS

1. Small cockroaches, 15 mm long or less, including tegmina 2
-- Large cockroaches, longer than 15 mm including tegmina 5

2. Pronotum with two longitudinal dark bars 3
-- Pronotum without two longitudinal dark bars 4

3. Face with black line between eyes ex-
    tending to mouth . . . . Field Cockroach,
                                                    Blattella vaga

-- Face without black line between eyes
    extending to mouth . . . . German Cockroach,
                                                    Blattella germanica

4. Tegmina covering about half of ab-
    domen; pronotum at least 6-7 mm wide . . . . . . Wood Cockroaches,
                                                    Parcoblatta spp.

-- Tegmina covering almost all of abdo-
    men (female) or extending beyond ab-
    domen (male); pronotum less than 6-7
    mm wide . . . . Brown-banded Cockroach,
                                                    Supella longipalpa

5. Large cockroaches, 15-55 mm including
    tegmina 6
-- Very large cockroaches, greater than 55
    mm including tegmina . . . . Blaberus spp.

6. Tegmina noticeably shorter than abdomen 7
-- Tegmina just reaching apex of abdomen
    or extending beyond 12

7. Tegmina fully covering metanotum 8
-- Tegmina extending beyond mesonotum
    but not fully covering metanotum 10

8. Pronotum with Lobster-like pattern . . . . Lobster Cockroach,
                                                    Nauphoeta cinerea

-- Pronotum of uniform color, or with
    lateral margins only pale 9

9. Female only, pronotal margins pale . . . . Wood Cockroaches,
                                                    Parcoblatta spp.

-- Male only, pronotum entirely uniform
    in color . . . . Oriental Cockroach,
                                                    Blatta orientalis

10. Pro-, meso- and metanota brown-black
    with striking yellow pattern . . . . Neostylopyga rhombifolia
-- Pro-, meso- and metanota not marked
    with yellow 11

11. Body length 25 mm or less (female only) . . . . Oriental Cockroach,
                                                    Blatta orientalis

-- Body length 30 mm or more (male or
    female) . . . . Eurycotis floridana

12. Pronotum 6-7 mm wide 13
-- Pronotum more than 6-7 mm wide 14

13. Hind margin of pronotum smoothly
curved . . . . Wood Cockroaches,
Parcoblatta spp.

-- Hind margin of pronotum strongly sinu-
ate, the posterior apex bluntly rounded . . . . . Surinam Cockroach,
Pycnoscelus surinamensis

14. Posterior half of tegmina distinctly
mottled with two pronounced dark
lines in the basal area . . . . Madeira Cockroach,
Leucophaea maderae

-- Tegmina not mottled or with dark lines
in the basal area 15

15. Base of tegmina with pale streak on
outer edges. Pronotum strikingly marked
with a dark central area and pale outer
edging (Fig. 1.9) . . . . Australian Cockroach,
Periplaneta australasiae

Base of tegmina without pale streak on
outer edges. Pronotum of uniform
color or with pale edging only moder-
ately conspicuous 16

16. Pronotum uniformly dark in color
(Fig. 1.9). Body color very dark brown
to black . . . . Smoky-brown Cockroach
Periplaneta fuliginosa

Pronotum not entirely uniform in
color, but with a pale edging moder-
ately conspicuous 17

17. Last segment of cercus twice as long as
wide . . . . American Cockroach
Periplaneta americana

-- Last segment of cercus less than twice as
long as wide . . . . Brown Cockroach,
Periplaneta brunnea

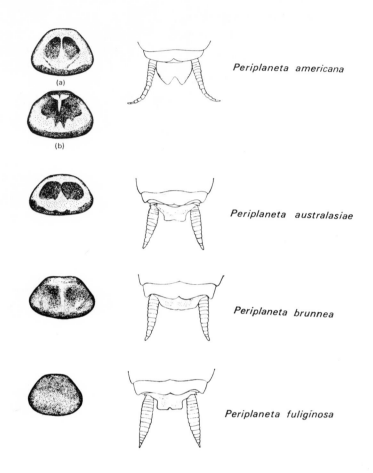

Fig. 1.9. Pronotal pattern and terminal abdominal segments (dorsal view) of males of four species of <u>Periplaneta</u>. (a) Normal coloration, and (b) maximum intensive coloration of pronotum of <u>P</u>. <u>americana</u>.

KEY TO THE OOTHECAE OF COCKROACHES MOST COMMONLY FOUND IN BUILDINGS (see Fig. 1.10)

1. Ootheca with obvious segmentation on ventral surface, length less than 6-7 mm 2
-- Ootheca without segmention on ventral surface, length more than 6-7 mm 3

2. With 16-20 segments, length of ootheca more than twice width . . . . German Cockroach, *Blattella germanica*
-- With 8-9 segments, length of ootheca less than twice width . . . . Brown-banded Cockroach, *Supella longipalpa*

3. Sides of ootheca with 8-9 raised areas just below keel 4
-- Sides of ootheca with 12-13 raised areas just below keel . . . . Australian Cockroach, *Periplaneta australasiae* Brown Cockroach *Periplaneta brunnea* Smoky-brown Cockroach, *Periplaneta fuliginosa*
(Oothecae of these species cannot be distinguished on external characters.)

4. Raised areas below keel nearly circular . . . . . Oriental Cockroach, *Blatta orientalis*
-- Raised areas below keel elongate . . . . American Cockroach, *Periplaneta americana*

ootheca with obvious segmentation

with about 18 segments,
length more than twice width

with about 8 segments,
length less than twice width

Blattella germanica
GERMAN COCKROACH

Supella supellectilium
BROWN-BANDED COCKROACH

ootheca without obvious segmentation

8-9 raised areas below keel

areas circular

areas elongate

Blatta orientalis
ORIENTAL COCKROACH

Periplaneta americana
AMERICAN COCKROACH

12-13 raised areas below keel

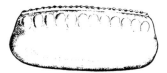

Periplaneta australasiae — AUSTRALIAN COCKROACH
Periplaneta brunnea — BROWN COCKROACH
Periplaneta fuliginosa — SMOKY-BROWN COCKROACH

Fig. 1.10. Oothecae of the most common species of cockroaches found in buildings (<u>Supella</u> <u>supellectilium</u> = <u>Supella</u> <u>longipalpa</u>).

Topic — 2 — COCKROACH CULTURE

It is true that cockroaches are very easy to maintain in the laboratory or classroom, and indeed they often live unassisted in these same types of environments. It is desirable, however, to adhere to the same rules of animal care for cockroaches that must be followed with other laboratory animals. In other words, even cockroaches should not be cultured unless they are cared for.

A. OBTAINING COCKROACHES CHEAPLY. Many species of cockroaches may be obtained by trapping or collecting; the rare species must be obtained from cockroach researchers or supply houses (Appendix II). Purchase of cockroaches from supply houses represents a relatively large investment if all of the specimens are to be used for dissection; the investment is less if the cockroaches purchased are used to initiate a reproducing colony.

Three species found nearly everywhere in the U.S. are Periplaneta americana, Blatta orientalis and Blattella germanica (see Figs. 1.1, 1.2 and 1.3). These can be trapped using quart or gallon jars coated on the inside with a thin layer of vaseline (petroleum jelly) and baited with banana and/or white bread dipped in beer. Excellent places for trapping are along walls or corners in kitchens, basements, and other warm places near food and water. Buildings where insecticide use is restricted are good places to trap: zoo buildings, aquaria, restaurants and cafeterias. In the Southern U.S. and in subtropical regions around the world it is possible to obtain, in a similar manner, Periplaneta fuliginosa, Periplaneta brunnea and Periplaneta australasiae. To locate Nauphoeta cinerea, Pycnoscelus surinamensis and Blaberus craniifer, the collector should trap near or in warehouses for fruit storage in Texas, Louisiana, Hawaii, Florida and neighboring states; in tropical regions B. craniifer will come to lights. Eurycotis floridana commonly occurs in outdoor sheds, on palm leaves, under logs and similar places in Florida and Central America. Nymphs occur in the leaf litter. Blattella vaga can be collected with a net in dry areas in S.W. U.S; nymphs occur in leaf litter. Parcoblatta and Ectobius occur in woodland and grassland in rural areas in most regions of the United States and Europe, respectively. Collect with a net during summer evenings. Nymphs are common in rotting wood, stacked firewood, and leaf litter during all seasons. Adults of some species are attracted to lights at night. Cryptocercus lives in oak hickory forest in N.W. U.S. and in the Appalacians. They make burrows in rotting wood; chopping open logs is the only way to find them. Arenivaga can be collected at night in desert areas; males are often attracted to lights.

B. COCKROACH CULTURE. The most efficient approach to culturing cockroaches is to raise only one or two species in large containers. This technique reduces maintenance to a minimum. Caring for several different species requires more time, although the resulting live collection offers more variety than one or two species.

From large cultures, which can be continued indefinitely, small groups of individuals can be removed periodically for classroom use. The minimum number of individuals required for constancy is 100. Fewer than 100 cockroaches tend to die off quickly or do not produce sufficient young to maintain a colony. If you have 100 Blatta orientalis or Periplaneta

15

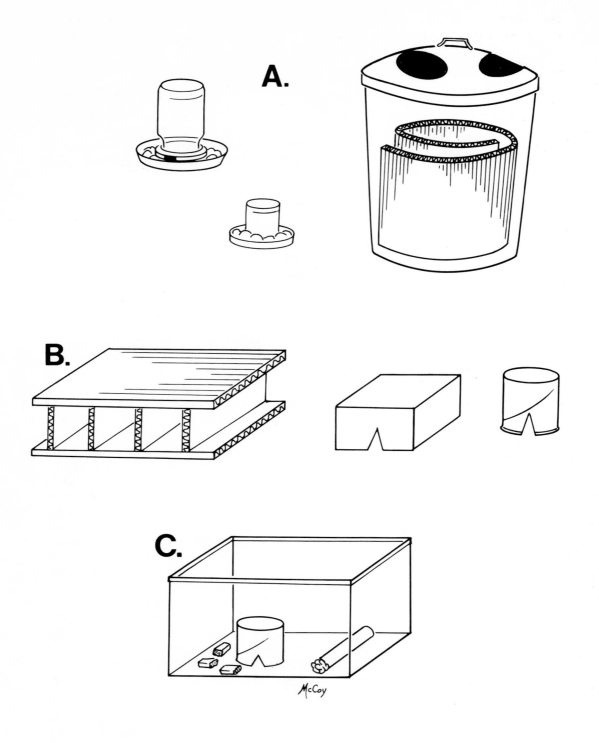

Fig. 2.1. (A) Trash can with screened lid and cardboard insert; beaker containing water inverted into a Petri dish (or 'chick-feeder'). (B) Cardboard shelters. (C) Aquarium set up for cockroaches; wood shavings, potted plants and branches of trees may be added.

americana and 50 of them are adult females, each female will produce about 16 nymphs every five days. That means nearly 500 nymphs per month and thousands of adults in less than one year! Not all will survive, of course, but the potential productivity is enormous.

Large colonies are best maintained in 50 gallon plastic or metal trash cans or 20 to 50 gallon aquaria. Both types of containers must have security lids and be stocked with cardboard or wooden harborages (Fig. 2.1). All cockroaches require crevices in which to hide during daylight hours, and so corrugated cardboard, egg cartons or other materials that increase surface area should be placed in colony containers. As shown in Fig. 2.1, the harborages must be arranged to allow for waterbottles and food.

Water can be provided in a variety of ways. The simplest device is a large test tube (30 x 200 mm) filled with water and capped with a wad of wet cotton. A 250 ml beaker of water inverted on a saucer or petri dish will also allow access to water. Both techniques require weekly changing, but larger test tubes or beakers will last longer.

To keep cockroaches in a metal trash can, you can set up an electric barrier about 10 to 15 cm from the top. Stick on a ring of cloth insulating tape and then a layer of aluminum tape on top of the insulator. Wire a 24-28 volt battery pack between the aluminum tape and the trash can itself. When a cockroach contacts both the can and the aluminum tape, it will receive a mild shock and jump back into the can.

Cockroaches are primarily omnivorous, and so feeding is quite simple. Most researchers use laboratory lab chow such as that used for rats, rabbits or hamsters. Most commercial dry dog foods will suffice, although for some reason the laboratory chows (Purina) are more stable at high humidity. It is important to keep lab chow in a sealed container to prevent entry of various beetles (on the other hand if the chow is not sealed it quickly provides a colony of another interesting type of insect to study). This basic diet may be augmented with apples, potatoes, or carrots to stimulate growth of contented, healthy, large specimens. Cockroach containers should be cleaned out only after 6 months or so (unless a problem develops). Our view of 'clean and healthy' differs from that of cockroaches.

C. <u>HANDLING COCKROACHES</u>. Handle cockroaches according to your index of queeziness. Forceps can be used with practice so that cockroaches are not damaged. Fingers are better (with plastic gloves if necessary). Allergic reactions to cockroaches are not uncommon, and if association with them causes sneezing and eye reactions, further handling should be curtailed.

D. REVERSING THE PHOTOCYCLE. Most cockroaches are nocturnal, and so it is necessary to maintain a reversed photocycle if cockroaches are to be maximally active during the daytime. A dark or fairly dark room outfitted with a 100 watt light and a utility timer will suffice. Simply provide 12 hours of light from about 6:00 p.m. to 6:00 a.m. and cockroaches will be active from about 8:00 a.m. to 4:00 p.m. However, many experiments can be performed even if reversing the photocycle is not practical. For some behavioral experiments, as indicated, it is best to work in reduced light if that is possible.

GENERAL READINGS

Siverly, R. E. 1962. Rearing Insects in Schools. Dubuque, Iowa: W. C. Brown Co.

Topic — **3** — OBSERVING COCKROACHES: AN INTRODUCTION TO THE BEAST

Pick up a cockroach from its container (large aquarium) and place it in a small jar for individual observation. If you use your hands you will feel a slight pricking sensation from the cockroach's tarsi (feet); this is caused by stiff claws on the tarsi that facilitate gripping the substratum during walking. In the observation jar the cockroach will probably run about excitedly and then it will calm down and remain in one place. Its next actions dispel the common belief that cockroaches are filthy creatures, for they will most likely groom and clean all legs, antennae and other parts of the body. What is the cockroach cleaning from its body?

Watch carefully to see what the cockroach does to inspect its environment. The palps and antennae will move constantly, tasting and smelling.

Next, observe several cockroaches placed together in a larger container (5 gallon aquarium) with or without the cardboard shelters from their home cage. Do cockroaches prefer open or sheltered areas? What does a cockroach do when it encounters another cockroach--how are the antennae used during these introductions and what information is gained? Are encounters 'friendly' or aggressive?

Observations of this kind may suggest experiments that are outlined in this book or that you will design and carry out on your own.

MATERIALS

Cockroaches (any species)
5-gallon aquarium

Several utility jars with screen or cloth tops (held by elastic bands)

Cardboard shelters from a colony (see Fig. 2.1)

NOTES TO INSTRUCTOR

1. Students must get close and have plenty of time to investigate cockroach habits.
2. This exercise may precede one or more of the anatomy or experimental exercises.
3. An excellent addition to this experiment is to have students develop a list of questions about cockroaches that come to mind during observational work.

Xestoblatta _hamata_, a large
Blattellid that looks like _Periplaneta_,
is commonly observed perching motionless on leaves 1 to 2 meters above
the rain forest floor. Nymphs, as
shown below, are spotted with yellow
and spend their time feeding on and
living in leaf litter on the forest
floor.

Topic—4—COCKROACH ANATOMY

In the warm, humid carboniferous period, 250 million years ago, cockroaches were probably the most numerous winged insects inhabiting the lush vegetation of that era. The fossil record shows that cockroaches millions of years ago had most of the same features which characterize modern cockroaches: large chewing mouthparts, antennae with many segments, large pronotum shielding the head, tough forewings and membranous hindwings heavily-spined walking legs and an abdomen with many similar segments. Morphologically, cockroaches are relatively unspecialized, not having, for example, modified legs for jumping or prey-catching, and not having evolved modifications for special kinds of flying or feeding . In fact, modern cockroaches are very similar to their ancestors, except that females no longer have elongated ovipositors for egg-laying and the wings are reduced or absent in many species.

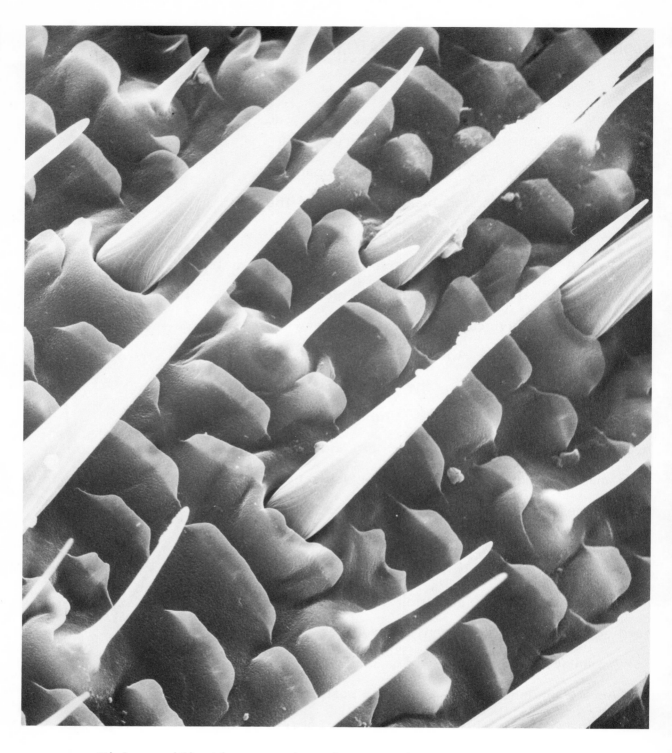

High magnification scanning electron micrograph of the surface of a cockroach antenna. Scale-like structures are outgrowths of epidermal cells. Two or three epidermal cells join to produce a sensory hair (sensillum) and the socket which supports the structure.

Exercise–4.1–EXTERNAL ANATOMY: CUTICULAR STRUCTURES

The cuticle of cockroaches is composed of 3 layers, secreted by cells of the epidermis. The outermost part is very thin, waxy and water repellent; the middle part is laminated and contains pigment; the inner layer is thick, pliable and sturdy. Together the layers of the cuticle protect the cockroach from water loss, provide a rigid, strong exoskeleton (the skeleton is on the outside) and areas of attachment inside for muscles. Epidermal cells not only secrete the cuticular layers, but also determine the types of structures (such as spines, hairs, eyes) that are constructed over the surface of the cockroach.

Anesthetize a cockroach and place it under a dissecting microscope. Examine the animal at low power, locating the head (notice the eyes and antennae), the thorax, where legs and wings attach, and the abdomen, the large posterior section (Fig. 4.1). Although cockroaches actually have up to 20 segments, homologous with the segments of earthworms, some segments have become fused and are difficult to distinguish.

Notice that appendages of the head (Fig. 4.2) and thorax (Figs. 4.3 and 4.4) are segmented. What is the function of the array of spines on the legs? Carefully examine the compound eyes, ocelli, and antennae under the microscope--are subcomponents visible? Fig. 4.5. shows a high power scanning micrograph of the sensory hairs on the cockroach antenna.

To investigate the appendages near the mouth, lift the labrum, and spread the maxillary palps (Figs. 4.6 and 4.7). The hard, shiny mandibles will now be exposed, above which is the mouth. If the cockroach is still alive, it will operate its mandibles and palps as you probe these appendages.

The thorax has three segments, prothorax with prothoracic legs, mesothorax with mesothoracic legs and forewings (tegmina) and metathorax with metathoracic legs and hind wings. The dorsal surfaces of these segments are termed pronotum, mesonotum and metanotum. Spiracles can be observed, as shown in Fig. 4.8.

The abdomen consists of 10 recognizable segments (count from the thorax posteriorly) (Fig. 4.9). Two plates comprise each segment, a dorsal tergum and ventral sternum. Squeeze the thorax to expand the abdomen, and observe the flexible intersegmental membranes that connect the plates in the anterior-posterior direction, and the pleural membranes connecting them dorso-ventrally. The system of plates and membranes is analogous to a hinged suit of armor (Fig. 4.10). At the tip of the abdomen are paired sensory organs, the cerci, which respond to puffs of wind and vibrations, and in males the styles which give tactile input during attempts to copulate. The last segments of the abdomen differ markedly between males and females; males have organs that evert during copulation and that grasp the female, whereas females have appendages used in oviposition and ootheca formation. Spiracles of the abdomen can be observed as shown in Fig. 4.8.

METHODS

Preserving insect parts on microscope slides: place tissue on a microscope slide, add a drop of Hoyer's solution or polyvinyl alcohol and a coverslip. Paint the edges of the coverslip with fingernail polish to seal the

BOX-1

MALE OR FEMALE?

The following cues and accompanying diagrams explain how to determine the sex of cockroaches:

(1) Blatta adults: males-wings, females-no wings
(2) Periplaneta adults: Fig. A.
(3) Blatta and Periplaneta nymphs: Fig. B.
(4) Blattella and Supella adults: males-longer, slender bodies, longer wings; females-stout bodies, shorter wings
(5) Blaberids (Leucophaea, Blaberus) adults: Fig. C.

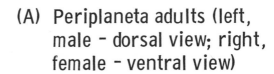

(A) Periplaneta adults (left, male - dorsal view; right, female - ventral view)

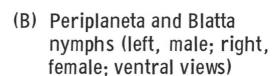

(B) Periplaneta and Blatta nymphs (left, male; right, female; ventral views)

(C) Blaberid adults (left, male; right, female; ventral views)

preparation. (Hoyers: mix 50 ml water, 30 g gum acacia or gum arabic, 200 g chloral hydrate, after 48 hours with intermittent stirring, add 20 g glycerol) Polyvinyl alcohol is more stable then Hoyers, and if mixed with phenol and lactic acid, will partially clear most tissues.

MATERIALS

Dissecting microscope
Dissecting instruments: forceps,
  small scissors, 2 probes,
  insect pins

Dissecting dish with wax or cork
  bottom

NOTES TO INSTRUCTOR

1. The information provided here can be supplemented with Guthrie and Tindall (1968), the most complete guide to the external anatomy of cockroaches.
2. Anesthetized cockroaches will become active again in about 5 min. Freezing them for 10 min. (which will kill them) may be necessary.

GENERAL READINGS

Andersen, S. O. 1979. Biochemistry of insect cuticle. Annu. Rev. Entomol. 24: 29-61.

Borror, D. J. and DeLong, D. M. 1971. An Introduction to the Study of Insects. New York: Holt, Rinehart and Winston.

Cornwell, P. B. 1968. The Cockroach, Vol. I. A Laboratory Insect and Industrial Pest. London: Hutchinson Press.

Guthrie, D. M. and Tindall, A. R. 1968. The Biology of the Cockroach. London: Edward Arnold Ltd. Chapter 2.

Richards, O.W. and Davies, R.G. 1977. Imms General Textbook of Entomology, 10th Edition; Vol. 1, Structure, Physiology and Development; Vol. 2, Classification and Biology. London: Chapman and Hall.

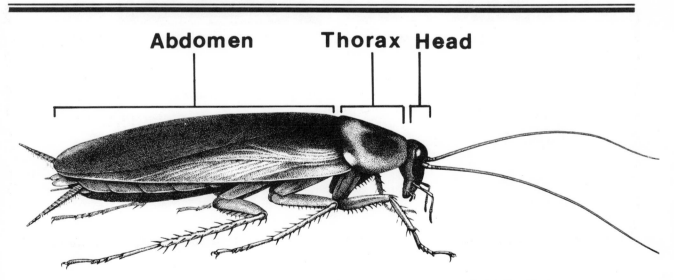

Abdomen   **Thorax Head**

Fig. 4.1. Male American cockroach, Periplaneta americana.

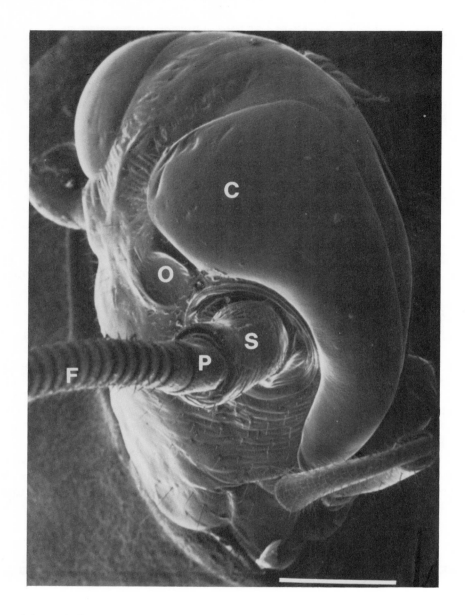

Fig. 4.2. Scanning electron micrograph of the cockroach head. C, compound eye; O, ocellus (simple eye); segments of the antenna, including S, scape; P, pedicel; F, flagellum. Bar = 1 mm.

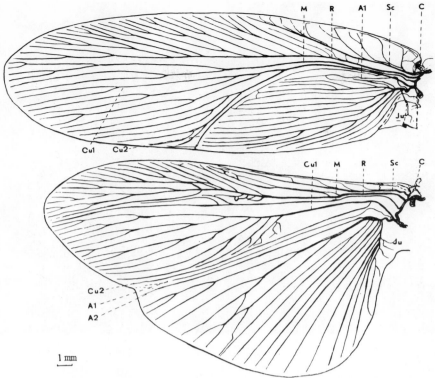

Fig. 4.3. Forewing (tegmen) and hindwing of _Periplaneta americana_. Abbreviations indicate the major veins of the wings, important characters for identifying uncommon species. The posterior portion of the hindwing is called the anal lobe. How do the wings fold up when not in use?

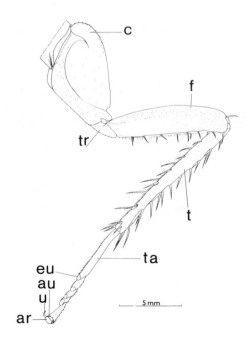

Fig. 4.4. Metathoracic leg of _Periplaneta americana_. Are the spines on the tibia positioned in exactly the same place in all of the individuals you have examined? c, coxa; tr, trochanter; f, femur; t, tibia; ta, tarsus; eu, euplantula; au, axilia; u, unguis; ar, arolium.

27

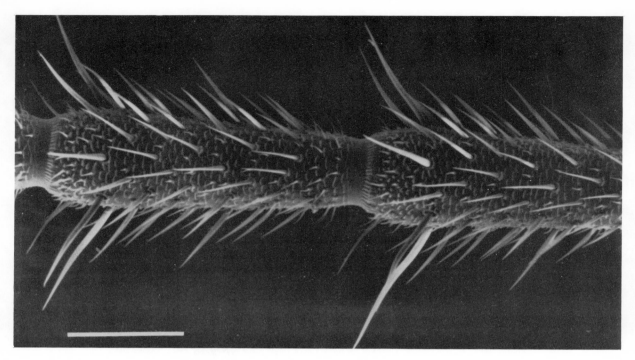

Fig. 4.5. Scanning electron micrograph of a cockroach antenna. Two segments or flagellomeres are shown with hair-like sensory sensilla. Bar = 125 μm.

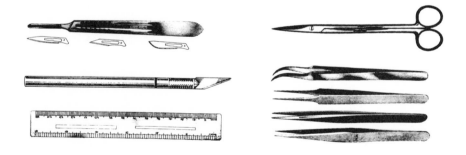

A selection of dissecting tools for experiments outlined in this book

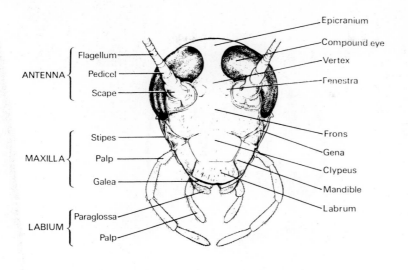

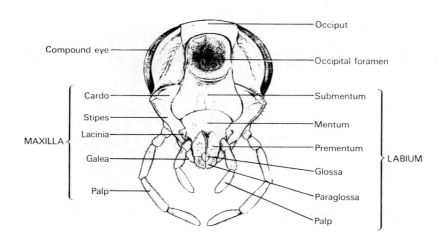

Fig. 4.6. Cockroach head and appendages, shown from the frontal view (above) and from behind (below). Note: the ocellus or simple eye is labelled 'fenestra' in this diagram.

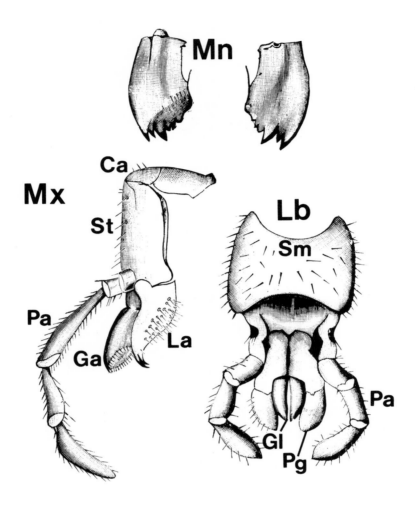

Fig. 4.7. Mouthparts of a cockroach viewed from behind (as in the lower diagram of Fig. 4.6). Mn, mandible; Mx, maxilla; Lb, labium; Gl, glossa; Pg, paraglossa; La, lacinia; Ga, galea; Pa, palp, Ca, cardo; St, stipes; Sm, submentum (mentum is just below).

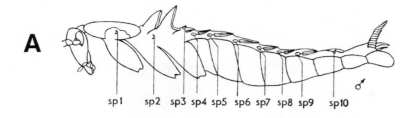

Fig. 4.8. (A) Spiracle distribution on the body of a male Blattella germanica, (B) Lateral view of tracheal system of a female Blattella germanica. SP, spiracle.

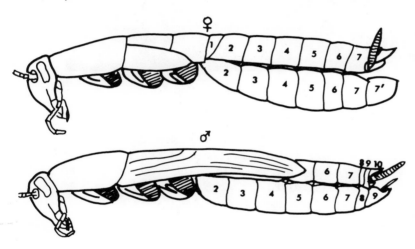

Fig. 4.9. Sideviews of female and male cockroaches indicating the abdominal segments.

Fig. 4.10. (A) Vertebrate skeletal joint showing endoskeleton with external muscle attachments. (B) Arthropod skeletal joint showing exoskeleton with internal muscle attachments. (C) Diagram of an arthropod limb extended, retracted and flexed.

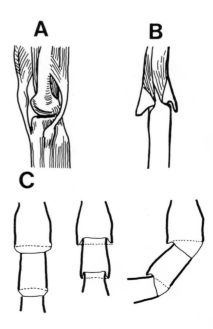

Enlargement of the antennal socket. Notice the scape-pedicel articulation and folded membrane within this joint that allow movement along an axis from the top right to the lower left of the photograph.

Exercise–4.2—INTERNAL ANATOMY: ORGAN SYSTEMS

Dissecting a cockroach is in some respects more challenging than dissecting a frog. With the aid of a dissecting microscope, however, the task is relatively simple.

Dissection can be accomplished with an anesthetized cockroach (see Box #2). Remove the legs and wings to inhibit movements during dissection. Now pin the cockroach, dorsal side up, to a wax or cork dish, placing the pins at the 'neck' and abdominal tip. Cut off the lateral abdominal and thoracic margins (about 1 mm) with scissors and remove the terga. The heart is attached to the abdominal terga, so try to keep them intact and in saline if possible.

Fig. 4.11 shows the major internal organs of a cockroach, and along with the following description, will serve as a dissecting guide. Remove the major organs as you work and place them in dishes of saline for closer observation under a dissecting microscope.

Examine the exposed organs and tissues to orient yourself relative to Fig. 4.11. The white, amorphous tissue filling much of the haemocoel (body cavity) is called fat body. The fat body is analogous in many ways to the vertebrate liver. Nutrients such as amino acids, fats and carbohydrates are stored in the fat body. Complex molecules such as proteins are synthesized by this tissue and secreted into the blood (also called haemolymph).

Embedded in the fat body are several obvious structures: components of the digestive system that run from the head to the posterior end; silvery white reproductive organs in the posterior part of the abdomen; and tracheae that appear as shiny tubes throughout the body. To expose these organs further, carefully remove some of the fat body.

Anteriorly, the oesophagus in the thorax opens into a crop in the abdomen which terminates at the proventriculus (or gizzard), containing a grinding apparatus of sclerotized teeth. Posterior to the proventriculus are several tube-like appendages, the gastric caecae (usually orange colored), that secrete enzymes for digestion and also participate in absorption of nutrients. The midgut (also called ventriculus) is where most chemical digestion and absorption of nutrients occurs. The hindgut is active primarily in absorption of salts and water; in the rectum, water is actively transported into the blood. Malpighian tubules, hair-like yellow excretory organs, enter the digestive tract near the junction of the midgut and hindgut. Salivary glands (two) and their reservoirs are found in the thorax, and are connected by a duct to the hypopharynx. The reservoirs are almost transparent, but can usually be seen if they are punctured and become folded.

The ovaries, in segments 4 to 6 (in P. americana), are conspicuous in mature females, as yellowish organs consisting of tubes of developing eggs called ovarioles (Fig. 4.12A). There are two ovaries, joining posteriorly in a common oviduct. The spermatheca, which stores sperm, connects to the oviduct, and is strategically positioned to allow sperm access to the eggs that move down the oviduct at the time of ootheca formation. Colleterial glands, which secrete substances that form the ootheca, open into the vestibulum of the genital pouch at the base of the ovipositor. Some

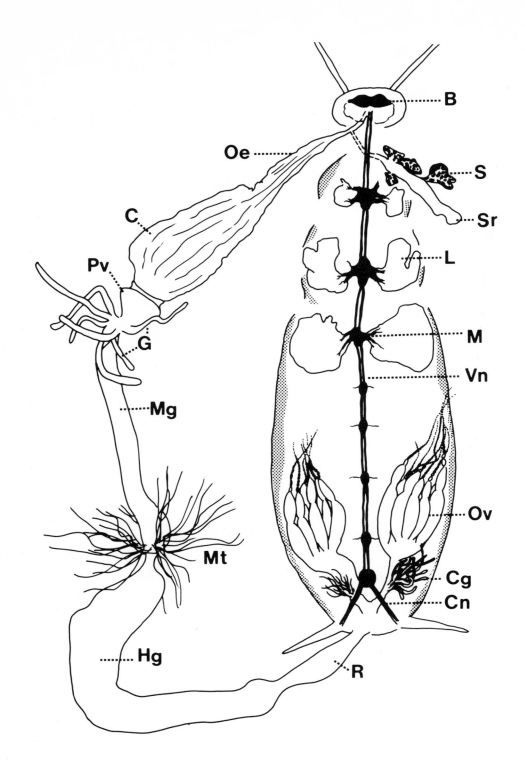

Fig. 4.11. Dissection of an adult female (*Periplaneta americana*, showing major organs. Oe, oesophagus; C, crop; Pv, proventriculus; G, gastric caecae; Mg, midgut (ventriculus); Mt, Malpighian tubules; Hg, hindgut; R, rectum; B, brain; S, salivary gland; Sr, salivary gland reservoir; L, leg muscle; Vn, ventral nerve cord; M, metathoracic ganglion; Ov, ovary; C, colleterial gland; Cn, cercal nerve.

cockroach species (Blaberids) have a <u>uterus</u>. The eggs are withdrawn into the body after ovulation and oviposition, and are incubated in the <u>uterus</u>.

The reproductive system of the male cockroach includes paired <u>testes</u> located dorsally approximately half way along the abdomen (segments 4 and 5 in <u>P</u>. <u>americana</u>) (Fig. 4.12B). <u>Sperm</u> move from the <u>vas</u> <u>deferens</u> canal, by way of the <u>vesiculae</u> <u>seminales</u>, to the <u>ejaculatory</u> duct. <u>Accessory glands</u>, often rich in uric acid, are important in forming a <u>spermatophore</u> - or sperm bundle - that is transferred through the ejaculatory duct to the female. The testes can be removed, cut into pieces in saline and viewed on a microscope slide at low power using a compound microscope. Living sperm cells can be observed.

A network of silvery tubes can be seen throughout the body. These tubes, silvery because of their air content, are the <u>tracheae</u>. They and their minute ramifications, the <u>tracheoles</u>, constitute the respiratory system. Air enters the system by way of 10 pairs of lateral openings, the <u>spiracles</u> (Fig. 4.13). Gaseous exchange is brought about by diffusion as air is moved into and out of the system by contraction and relaxation of the abdominal muscles. Grasp one of the large tracheae with forceps and pull--notice that tracheae are reinforced by coiled fibers (<u>taenidia</u>) (Fig. 4.14). Mount a piece of this material in a drop of water on a microscope slide and examine with a compound microscope. Trace a few of the larger tracheae to smaller ones. To see the tracheoles, remove a sample of fat body and add 0.5% methylene blue on a microscope slide; examine the slide under a compound microscope.

The <u>central</u> <u>nervous</u> <u>system</u> of a cockroach consists of a brain (above the oesophagus), <u>suboesophageal</u> <u>ganglion</u> (below the oesophagus), and a <u>ventral</u> <u>nerve</u> <u>cord</u> (looks like dual threads) (Fig. 4.15). Along the ventral nerve cord are nine smaller ganglia. The cord can be observed most easily after the digestive system, fat body and reproductive system have been removed. Nerves are almost transparent, however, and are difficult to see. The <u>brain</u>, which fills most of the head capsule, receives neurons from the sense organs of the head, and is also connected posteriorly by neurons to two major endocrine glands, the <u>corpora</u> <u>cardiaca</u> and <u>corpora</u> <u>allata</u> (Fig. 4.16); these can be observed if the dorsal part of the 'neck' is opened and the large tracheae removed. A <u>visceral</u> <u>nervous</u> <u>system</u> extends from the anterior end of the ventral nerve cord along the length of the digestive system.

The <u>dorsal</u> <u>blood</u> <u>vessel</u>--which in the abdomen is called the heart--runs along the dorsal midline just below the cuticle. This was removed at the beginning of the dissection, and should be examined now. Blood flows anteriorly towards the head and also laterally through small, short vessels (<u>ostia</u>). The blood then moves posteriorly in the <u>haemocoel</u> . Accessory pumps are located at the bases of the wings, legs and antennae to move blood through these small diameter organs. <u>Blood</u> <u>cells</u> (<u>haemocytes</u>) of cockroaches function in phagocytosis (incorporation of foreign or damaged tissue), hormone transport, wound healing and coagulation.

Muscles, which appear as pink or brown structures, are especially noticeable in the thorax, where those of the wings are located. Some leg muscles are located here as well.

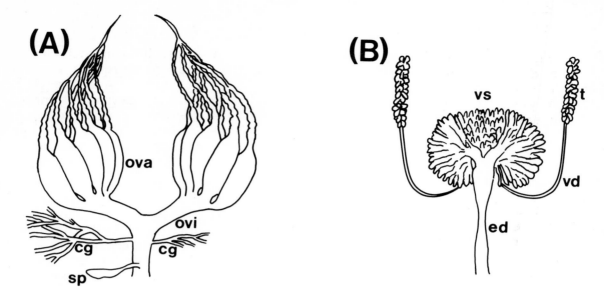

Fig. 4.12. Reproductive system of a female (A) and male (B) cockroach (generalized). Ova, ovaries (2) composed of ovarioles; ovi, oviduct; cg, colleterial glands (left and right); sp, spermatheca; t, testis (appears larger in the animal, owing to fat body embedded around each lobe); vd, vas deferens; ed, ejaculatory duct; vs, vesiculae seminales, located within the large mass of tubules which are male accessory glands or utriculi.

Fig. 4.13. Major tracheae of a cockroach (dorsal view). Closed circles represent spiracles.

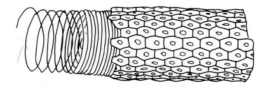

Fig. 4.14. Diagram of trachea showing external epidermis covering helical-shaped taenidia.

MATERIALS

Cockroaches (large adults of both
  sexes)
Dissecting microscope, dissecting
  dish and instruments
Glass dishes or Petri dishes
0.5% methylene blue (0.5 g dye,
  100 ml saline)

Cockroach saline: Add the following to 800 ml distilled water:
  9.32 g NaCl, 0.77 g KCl, 0.18 g
  $NaHCO_3$, 0.01 g NaH_2PO_4; when
  all crystals are dissolved, add
  0.5 g $CaCl_2$; stir well, and bring
  volume to 1000 ml. Keep in
  refrigerator if possible

NOTES TO INSTRUCTOR

1. This exercise is a prerequisite for all experiments in Topic 5 and can
    easily be combined in one session with one or two of the experiments in
    Topic 5.
2. Use the largest cockroaches available: Periplaneta, Leucophaea or
    Blaberus are recommended.

GENERAL READINGS

Chapman, R. F. 1969. The Insects. Structure & Function. New York:
  Elsevier.
Smith, D. S. 1968. Insect cells: Their structure and function.
  Edinburgh: Oliver and Boyd.

BOX-2

COCKROACH ANESTHESIA. METHOD 1: 'Cool down' the cockroach for 10 to 15 minutes in a refrigerator; freezing will kill
it. METHOD 2: Immerse the cockroach under warm water for
5 minutes; much longer is required for drowning. METHOD 3:
Pipe carbon dioxide into the container holding the cockroach
for 2 minutes; CO_2 can be tapped from a compressed gas tank
or from dry ice. (ETHER FUMES ARE NOT RECOMMENDED.)

Fig. 4.15. Central nervous system of a cockroach. From anterior to posterior: sup, supraoesophageal ganglion (brain); sub, suboesophageal ganglion; hole in center is where oesophagus passes through; th, thoracic ganglia; a, abdominal ganglia.

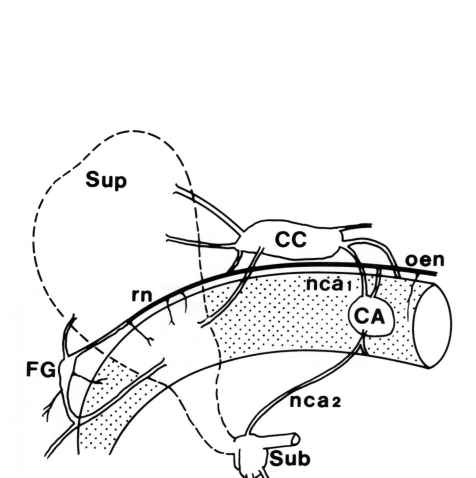

Fig. 4.16. Sideview of the nervous system in the head. Dashed outline in upper left indicates position of brain and circumoesophageal connective (circling the oesophagus); CC, corpus cardiacum; CA, corpus allatum; Sup, supraoesophageal ganglion; Sub, suboesophageal ganglion; nca 1, 2, nervi corporis cardiaci (nerves); FG, frontal ganglion; rn, recurrent nerve; oen, oesophageal nerve.

Topic —5— PHYSIOLOGICAL EXPERIMENTS

Once you have studied cockroach morphology and have learned how to handle the beast, the following physiological experiments can be attempted. A worthwhile approach is to realize that all animals have very similar problems to solve in obtaining and utilizing nutritional resources, moving in and responding to the environment, and successfully reproducing. The cockroach reveals unique physiological adaptations to solve these problems, but at the same time, many of the solutions are common to or similar to those of other organisms that you have already studied or will study in the future.

Megaloblatta *blaberoides* (Blattellidae) *nymph beside a U.S. 25¢ piece (25 mm diameter). These nymphs produce stridulatory alarm noises when disturbed by predators. Adults are 10 cm in length and are good fliers.*

Exercise-**5.1**—NUTRITION: FOOD MANIPULATION AND DIGESTION

Cockroaches that are capable of inhabiting our houses are omnivorous, perhaps as a preadaptation for this style of living. Most cockroaches are not omnivorous, however, and feed on algae, fungi or fruit. The purpose of the following experiments is to observe feeding, trace the ingested food material, and investigate certain aspects of digestion.

A. FEEDING. Observe cockroaches (deprived of food for 2 to 3 days) approach and ingest food. Notice that the legs are not involved, but that appendages near the mouth are very active. Anesthetize a cockroach, remove its legs and restrain it on its back using modeling clay. Roll a small (2 mm) piece of moist white bread dough in congo red stain (or powdered litmus). Place the 'food' on the mouth area and slip the animal under a dissecting microscope. How does the animal move and manipulate the food? How many appendages are involved and how do they work together?

After the cockroach has consumed as much as it will take, offer a few drops of water, during the next 24 hours you can observe the movement of the dye through the digestive system. Because you have used pH indicators as dyes, the pH of the gut organs can be estimated by color changes of the indicator. Does food move at a constant rate or does it remain in some organs longer than others?

If you examine samples of material from the crop and the midgut (under the microscope), you will note a marked reduction in particle size. Carefully dissect open the proventriculus to expose the 'teeth' responsible for grinding food material that passes into the midgut. How does this apparatus work? In the examination of gut contents suggested above it is probable that you will discover a few unexpected organisms that live in the cockroach gut. Can you identify these organisms? Speculate on why they live in this environment and the possible nutritional contribution they make to the cockroach?

B. DIGESTIVE ENZYMES. By assaying for enzymes in each organ of the gut, you can further delineate the functions of these organs. The data from enzyme tests can be either qualitative (yes-no) or quantitative (how much enzyme activity), depending on which of the enzyme assays you carry out. DATA BLANK II will have to be modified if you gather quantitative data. Some planning will also be necessary, as several assays should proceed simultaneously!

(1) Proteases. Enzymes that digest proteins, breaking down these large molecules into amino acids, will digest the gelatin on the emulsion side (dull side) of exposed and developed, photographic film. Cut each organ in the digestive tract and place a drop of fluid or material from each part onto a piece of film. Place the film in a container with moist cotton, so that the liquid will not dry out, but also so that water from the cotton will not seep onto the film. After about 45 minutes, wash the film in tap water. Hold the film up to the light--if a transparent spot is evident where the drop was positioned, the drop contains enzymes capable of digesting proteins.

(2) Invertase. Invertase breaks down complex sugars, such as sucrose, into simple sugars, such as fructose or glucose. The assay described below will provide an opportunity for the invertase in each organ

==

DATA BLANK I. Results of experiments with digestive organs

Organ	Function(s)	pH	Particle size
oesophagus			
salivary glands			
crop			
proventriculus			
gastric caeca			
midgut			
hindgut			

==

==

DATA BLANK II. Results of enzyme tests

Organ		Protease	Amylase	Invertase
oesophagus				
salivary glands				
crop				
proventriculus				
gastric caeca				
midgut				
hindgut				

==

NOTES:

A blank is provided in case you are able to analyze lipases, which digest fats and lipids.

NOTES:

Particle size determinations can be based on measurements using a micrometer grid with a compound microscope, a series of sieves, or you can estimate particle size.

of the gut to break down sucrose into fructose and glucose; a colored precipitate will indicate the presence of simple sugars, and an additional manipulation will dissolve the precipitate for quantitative measurement of the precipitate in a spectrophotometer. Note that the salivary glands are prime candidates for the invertase assay.

Remove each organ of the gut (pool the organs from several cockroaches to provide sufficient material), and homogenize (or grind) in saline, using just enough saline to facilitate homogenization. Allow the material to settle in a test tube, or centrifuge to produce a clear supernatant.

Prepare several tubes with 1.0 ml of 5% sucrose, and add 0.2 ml of each supernatant to a sucrose tube; if 0.2 ml is more than you have prepared, add less supernatant, but be sure to use the same amount of supernatant from each homogenate. Place the tubes in a waterbath at 35°C for 1 hour.

Mix 0.5 ml of Nelson's reagent part A with 12.5 ml of part B; shake. Pipette 1.0 ml of Nelson's mixture into each of several tubes and add 1.0 ml from each of the cooled sucrose tubes; shake. You should now have one tube with Nelson's mixture for each gut organ and a control with saline only. Place all of the Nelson's mixture tubes in boiling water (in a 500 ml beaker) for exactly 20 min. Remove and place in a beaker of cold water. A brown precipitate will be noticeable in those tubes that contained simple sugars, indicating which gut organs contain invertase.

For quantitative determination of enzymes, add 1.0 ml arsenomolybdate reagent to each Nelson's mixture tube and shake occasionally for 5 min to dissolve the precipitate. When dissolved, add 7.0 ml distilled water. Pipette the blue colored solutions into spectrophotometer tubes and measure the density of the color in a spectrophotometer at 540 mμ against a sucrose blank. To determine the amount of simple sugar that produces a given level of color density you will have to prepare standards with known amounts of sugar, and then follow the above procedure. Prepare test tubes containing 1.0 ml of Nelson's mixture, and then add the following amounts of glucose solution (100 μg/ml) and distilled water:

Tube number:	1	2	3	4	5	6
Distilled water (ml):	0	0.2	0.4	0.6	0.8	1.0
Glucose (100 μg/ml) (ml):	1.0	0.8	0.6	0.4	0.2	0.0

Obtain density readings on the spectrophotometer. Now you can quantify the optical density readings obtained with the gut homogenates in terms of μg simple sugar.

(3) Amylase. Starches are broken down to simple sugars by amylases. To test for this class of enzyme, add 0.3 ml of gut supernatant to 1.0 ml of 1% soluble starch solution in test tubes. Shake well and leave the tubes for 1 hour at 25°C. Test the solutions for simple sugars using the same procedure as in section (2) above, to determine what organs of the gut contain enzymes that break down starches.

C. STOMACH CONTENT ANALYSIS. Cockroaches seem to be omnivorous--at least in houses they eat almost anything. What are their food preferences in nature? Capture 'wild' cockroaches as described on page 15 and dissect open the gut. Put a drop of gut material on a microscope slide with a drop of glycerin and study the material with a compound microscope. Can you identify plant or animal tissues?

43

D. <u>NUTRITION AND DIET</u>. Cockroaches will readily feed on most any diet that you prepare for them. Cockroach 'cubes' can be manufactured by mixing known sources of protein (soy, gelatin), carbohydrate (starch, sugar), lipids (cholesterol, fatty acids), salts, vitamins and water; after drying in a mold, these can be fed to cockroaches. Two effects of diet that might be tested are (1) survival, and (2) ability of females to produce egg cases (refer to Exercise 5.4).

METHODS

<u>Nelson's reagent</u> <u>A</u>. 7.5 g $CuSO_4 \cdot 5H_2O$ in 50 ml water; add 1 drop of concentrated H_2SO_4; <u>B</u>. Dissolve 12.5 g Na_2CO_3 (anhydrous), 12.5 g potassium sodium tartrate, 10 g $NaHCO_3$ and 100 g Na_2SO_4 (anhydrous) in 500 ml water.

<u>Arsenomolybdate solution</u> - Dissolve 25 g $(NH_4)_6 \cdot Mo_7O_{24} \cdot 4H_2O$ in 450 ml water; add 21 ml concentrated H_2SO_4. Dissolve 3 g $Na_2HAsO_4 \cdot 7H_2O$ in 25 ml water and add to above. Store in a dark bottle for 24 hr at 37°C. The solution should be yellow, with no green tint.

NOTE: All solutions given in % refer to grams per 100 ml water or saline (e.g., 1% sucrose = 1 g/100 ml).

MATERIALS

Cockroaches (large adults);
  captured cockroaches from outdoors
Dissecting microscope; dissecting
  dish and instruments
Modeling clay or Tackiwax
White bread
Compound microscope (optional);
  microscope slides and coverslips

Congo red stain (powdered) or
  powdered litmus
Exposed, developed photographic
  film (black)
Cotton
Saline
Glycerin

<u>Materials for optional</u>
  <u>quantitative assays</u>:

Nelson's reagent
Arsenomolybdate solution
5% sucrose
1% soluble starch
Glucose soln (100 µg/ml)

Spectrophotometer and tubes
Water bath
500 ml beaker
Pipettes (1 and 10 ml)
Homogenizers
Test tubes (10 ml)

NOTES TO INSTRUCTOR

1. To locate micro-organisms in the gut, a low-power compound microscope is required.

2. Refer to page 15 for collecting 'wild' cockroaches.

3. Grasshoppers can be used in these experiments as a substitute for cockroaches, or for comparison.

GENERAL READINGS

Abbott, R. L. 1926. Contributions to the physiology of digestion in the Australian roach, Periplaneta australasiae. J. exp. Zool. 44:219-225.

Bignell, D. E. 1981. Nutrition. In: The American Cockroach, Ed. by W. J. Bell and K. G. Adiyodi. London: Chapman & Hall.

Dadd R. H. 1970. Digestion in insects. In: Chemical Zoology, Vol. 5, Ed. by M. Florkin and B. T. Scheer. New York: Academic Press.

House, H. L. 1974. Nutrition. In: The Physiology of Insecta, Vol. 5, Ed. by M. Rockstein. New York: Academic Press.

Neville , A. C. 1975. Biology of the Arthropod Cuticle. Berlin: Springer.

RESEARCH REPORTS

Bignell, D. E. 1976. Gnawing activity, dietary carbohydrate deficiency and oothecal production in the American cockroach (Periplaneta americana). Experientia 32: 1405-1406.

Qadri, S. S. and T. B. Rao. 1963. On a new flagellate Polymastix periplaneta from the common cockroach Periplaneta americana. Riv. Parasitol. 24: 153-158.

Snipes , B. T. and O. E. Tauber. 1937. Time required for food passage through the alimentary tract of the cockroach Periplaneta americana. Annals Entomol. Soc. Amer. 30: 277-284.

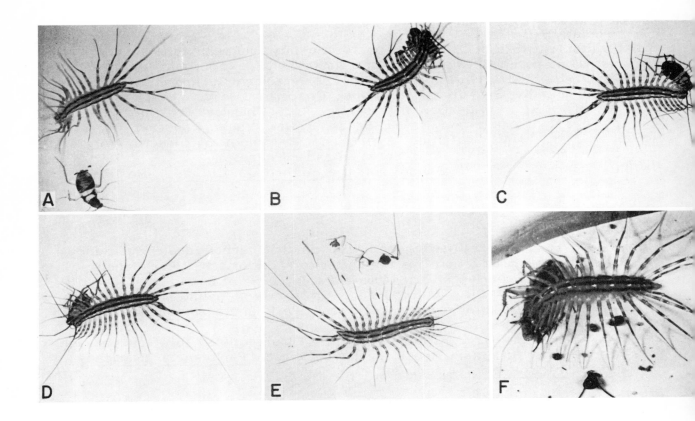

The centipede *Scutigera coleoptrata* capturing and feeding on cockroaches in the laboratory. A-E, pursuit, capture and eating of a nymph of *Supella longipalpa*. F, centipede feeding on an adult *Blattella germanica*.

Exercise-5.2—CIRCULATION AND EXCRETION

The circulatory system of cockroaches has several functions, including transport of nutrients, waste products, and hormones; blood cells are involved in coagulation, wound healing and immune responses. Oxygen is not circulated in the blood, as insects pump oxygen-containing air directly to the body tissues through the spiracles and the tracheal system.

Your dissection of a cockroach clearly showed a lack of blood vessels as we know them in vertebrates. Thus blood circulation in cockroaches is referred to as an 'open system' in which all of the organs are bathed in blood within the haemocoel. Although the cockroach heart is a relatively weak organ, it suffices to move the blood through the body and is assisted by auxiliary pumps at the base of the antennae, legs and wings.

Excretory organs, primarily the Malpighian tubules, are diffuse, hairlike organs that are spread through most of the abdomen. This is just the opposite of our own excretory system in which all of the blood is driven through the kidney, where filtering action regulates salt concentration and removes impurities from the blood. Other tissues are also involved in the removal of foreign particles and molecules in the blood, as will be illustrated in the following experiments.

A. DYE INJECTION TO ILLUSTRATE CIRCULATION AND EXCRETION. By injecting various dyes and other substances into a cockroach we can observe circulation of these indicators through the body and determine how they are removed from the blood. Four excellent dyes are trypan blue, neutral red, indigo carmine and India ink. These solutions are injected into the leg or abdomen of a cockroach (see Box #3). Both males and females should be used for observing uptake of the dye; for circulation, newly molted 'tan' individuals work best. Depending on where you make the injection you can follow the flow of the dye particles as they move through the body. A 'map' can be generated showing the overall pattern of circulation. By dissecting the animals 10 min, 30 min, 2 hrs, 6 hrs and 24 hrs after injection you can trace the uptake of the dye by excretory organs, tissues and cells. What are the major excretory organs (or tissues) and by what routes do they rid the body of wastes? How quickly are dye particles eliminated? Are dye particles also taken up by reproductive and digestive organs?

B. EXCRETION IN VITRO. Remove 2 or 3 Malpighian tubules in a few drops of saline containing neutral red or indigo carmine. Watch to see if the dye particles are taken up by the tubules, and if so, what portions of the tubules are most active in this process. If you cut open a tubule after 1 hour, does it contain more dye than an equal volume of the original solution?

C. BLOOD CELLS. Anesthetize a cockroach (see Box #2) and fix it to a dissecting dish with modeling clay. Use clay also to position one antenna on a microscope slide. Focus the dissecting microscope on the tip of the antenna. Cut off the tip of the antenna and gently squeeze the cockroach to force some blood out of the wound. How long does it take for a clot to form? Stain the clotted blood cells with 1% Iodine to see the projections of these cells. Collect another sample of blood, but this time add the blood onto a drop of mineral oil to prevent clotting. Examine the blood cells under a microscope. Can you estimate the number of cells per microliter? Stain a sample with Giemsa stain to clearly view the blood cells.

Collect a sample of blood with a micropipette from an animal that you previously injected with India ink. Put a drop of this blood on a microscope slide, add a coverslip, and examine under a compound microscope. What function for insect blood cells is suggested by the India ink particles that can be seen inside the cells?

D. RATE OF HEARTBEAT. We know that the human heart beats faster or more slowly, depending on the demand for increased or decreased blood pressure. For example, a frightening experience immediately causes your heart to beat very fast. This is true for many other animals as well. In the following exercises you will determine to what extent the cockroach heart responds to environmental changes and other factors.

Three kinds of preparations will be used: (i) an intact cockroach, (ii) the heart attached to the dorsal terga (see Exercise 4.2) and placed in saline, and (iii) a portion of the heart removed from the terga and placed in saline.

(1) Normal rate of heartbeat. Place several small vials (~ 2×8 cm) in a cage of cockroaches the day before your experiment (nymphs work best because they have no wings to shield the heart). Some of the residents will probably hide in vials, providing an opportunity for you to see and measure their heartbeat without disturbing them. Place the entire cage under a low power dissecting microscope and focus onto a cockroach resting

BOX-3

INJECTING COCKROACHES: Attach the needle to the syringe and draw up the solution to be injected. Hold the syringe, needle pointing upwards, and expel a small quantity of solution (and trapped air) into a wad of cotton. LEG METHOD: Bend the femur-tibia joint to expose the membrane. Insert the needle through the membrane into the femur and inject the solution. As the needle is withdrawn, pull the femur-tibia joint closed (to a straight position) to prevent bleeding. ABDOMEN METHOD: Use the same basic technique as with the leg, but insert the needle dorsally, through the intersegmental membrane, to the left or right of the midline. Run the needle anteriorly against the integument, preventing damage to internal organs. Inject the solution and withdraw the needle.

in a vial. Use a stopwatch to count the number of beats for a 5 min. period. Repeat this exercise for several individuals and calculate the mean (average) heartrate in beats per min. Record these values in DATA BLANK I.

(2) Stress. Remove the cockroaches from their vials and restrain them dorsal side up with modeling clay. Quickly begin recording the rate of heartbeat as soon as you have them in an immobile position. Is the rate of heartbeat altered by this potentially stressful situation of being captured and restrained? To add more stress, shine a bright light on the cockroaches. Turn off the light. After 30 min. does the rate of heartbeat return to control (normal) levels?

(3) Effects of feeding. Inject the restrained cockroach with 50 µl of 15% glucose to simulate the digestion of a meal. What effect does this have on the rate of heartbeat? How long does the effect last?

(4) Isolated heart preparation. Dissect the dorsal sclerites from the body, with the heart intact and still attached (see Exercise 4.2). Pin this preparation to a wax bottom dish so that you can see the heart under a low

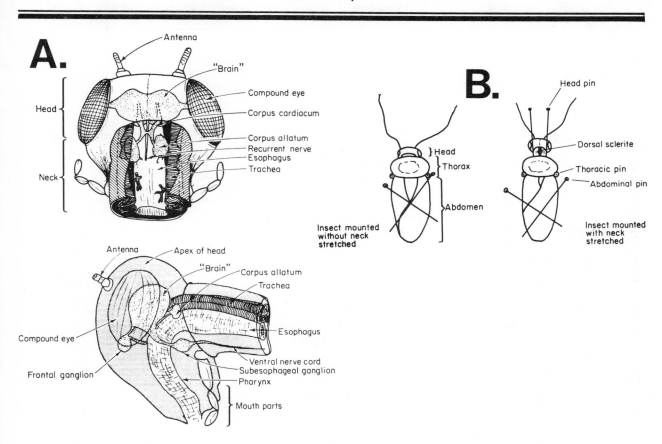

Fig. 5.1. (A) Dorsal and sideview of surgical approach for removing the corpora allata and corpora cardiaca from a cockroach. (B) Preparation of a cockroach for surgery; pins are placed just posterior to the head, stretching the neck forward to expose the cervical sclerites.

==

DATA BLANK I. Rate of heartbeat

Experiments			Average (beats per min)
Intact animal	Resting cockroach		
	Stressed cockroach	1 min	
		30 min	
	10% glucose	1 min	
		30 min	
	Saline control	1 min	
		30 min	
Isolated terga with heart attached	10% glucose		
	CO_2-saline		
	Saline control		
Isolated heart segment	10% glucose		
	CO_2-saline		
	Saline control		

==

NOTES:

(1) Rate of heartbeat in some species, under some circumstances, might be periodic rather than continuous. In that case you may have to quantify the time between bursts of heartbeats. The periodicity can also be graphed.

(2) To compare averages between experiments, use the t-test, a statistical measure discussed in Appendix I.

power dissecting microscope. Add a few drops of saline. Record the rate of beating of the isolated heart. Is it more like the rate for the resting or the stressed intact cockroach? Add 10% glucose; what is the response? If you have a source of carbon dioxide, bubble the gas through saline for several minutes, and then apply some of the carbon dioxide-saline to the heart; this might be similar to conditions characteristic of intense exercise. Does the heart beat faster, attempting to circulate the blood more quickly throughout the body?

(5) <u>Hormones</u>. The major cockroach hormones are secreted by the corpus allatum (CA) and corpus cardiacum (CC), tiny endocrine glands just posterior to the brain (Fig. 4.16). Dissecting out these glands is fairly difficult, but if you persist, it can be done. You will need a dissecting microscope, fine watchmaker's forceps and a cockroach anesthetized and immoblized with clay. Arrange the head so that the mandibles of the cockroach are tucked down towards its forelegs (Fig. 5.1). The dorsal cervical area (neck) must be exposed. Pull off the membranous dorsal sclerites from the head capsule posteriorly. Remove the large trachaea that are now exposed. The CA and CC can be observed lying on top of the oesophagus with nerves attaching them to the brain. Usually they appear as bluish to white lobes. Grasp the nerve connections and gently pull the glands free.

Crush or homogenize the glands (as many as you can obtain) in saline and apply the saline and glands to the dorsal sclerite preparation. What is the effect of the released hormones over a 30 min. period? If you can differentiate between the CA and CC, determine which gland contributes the active substance.

(6) <u>Source of heartbeat signals</u>. Carefully dissect out one segment of the heart (about 3-5 mm) in length, and place it in 0.1 ml saline. When it rests on the bottom of the dish, focus with a dissecting microscope to see if this small part of the heart is still beating? Will any segment of the heart do the same thing? If you have 5 such pieces in a dish, do they beat in unison? Can you change the rate of heartbeat in isolated segments with CO_2-saline, 10% glucose or hormones?

Reviewing your data from DATA BLANK I, can you develop a theory to explain how the rate of heartbeat is controlled in the cockroach? For example, do stimuli inside and/or outside the body influence the heart directly or through the nervous and endocrine systems?

MATERIALS

Cockroaches (<u>Periplaneta</u>; other species can be used for comparison); a few newly molted animals are needed in addition to adults.
Dissecting microscope
Compound microscope
Dissecting dish and instruments (including watchmaker's forceps)
Microscope slides
Disposable syringes (2 ml) and needles (24-28 gauge)
Mineral oil

Giemsa stain (Air dry a drop of blood on a slide; fix in absolute methanol 1 min; air dry; add a drop or two of stain diluted 1:10 in saline; after 30 min rinse in distilled water; air dry.)
10% trypan blue (10 g in 100 ml saline)
2% neutral red (2 g in 100 ml saline)
1% indigo carmine (1 g in 100 ml saline)
1% iodine (1 g in 100 saline)
India ink
Stop watch

10% glucose (10 g in 100 ml saline)
Water bath (or similar device)
Source of CO_2

NOTES TO INSTRUCTOR

1. Trypan blue, indigo carmine and India ink are difficult to remove from fingers, desks, etc.
2. Inject about one drop (50 µl of dye solution into each cockroach. Use only one kind of dye for each animal. India ink demonstrates circulation; trypan blue is slowly taken up by organs such as the ovaries, and often stimulates elimination of water; indigo carmine is removed from the blood by the Malpighian tubules within 30 min.
3. Refer to any physiology lab manual for instructions on analysis of blood consitituents by electrophoresis and other methods.
4. Further experiments on the cockroach heart, involving electrophysiological recording, are presented by McCann (1969); methods are outlined in Miller (1979).

GENERAL READINGS

Fox, P.M. 1981. Circulation. In: The American Cockroach, Ed. by W. J. Bell and K. G. Adiyodi. London: Chapman & Hall.

Jones, J. C. 1977. The Circulatory System of Insects. Springfield: Charles C. Thomas.

McCann, F. V. 1969. In: Experiments in Physiology and Biochemistry, Vol. 2, Ed. by G. A. Kerkut. New York: Academic Press.

Miller, T. A. 1974. Electrophysiology of the insect heart. In: The Physiology of Insecta, Vol. 4, Ed. by M. Rockstein. New York: Academic Press.

Miller, T. A. 1979. Insect Neurophysiological Techniques. Heidelberg: Springer-Verlag.

Mullins, D.E. 1981. Osmoregulation. In: The American Cockroach, Ed. by W.J. Bell and K.G. Adiyodi. London: Chapman & Hall.

RESEARCH REPORTS

Miller, T. A. 1979. Nervous versus neurohormonal control of insect heartbeat. Amer. Zool. 19:77-86.

Moran, D. T. 1971. Fine structure of cockroach blood cells. Tiss. & Cell 3:413-422.

Pichon, Y. and Boistel, J. 1968. Ionic composition of haemolymph and nervous function in the cockroach, Periplaneta americana. J. exp. Biol. 49:31-38.

Ramsay, J.A. 1955. The excretory system of the stick insect, Dixippus morosus. J. exp. Biol. 32:183-199.

NOTES:

The sketch shown below illustrates how to connect a tank of compressed carbon dioxide to a dissecting dish. This method keeps the cockroach under anesthesia during your operation in the exercises discussed here and in other chapters.

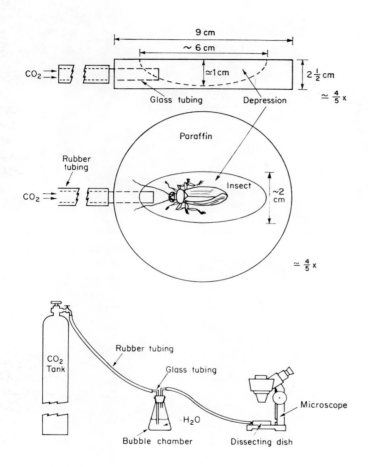

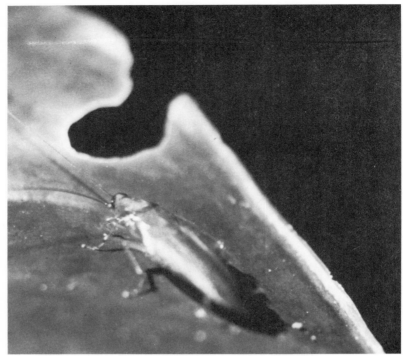

Epilampra sp. is a quick flier, often captured 2 to 3 meters above the rain forest floor. The genus belongs in the family Blaberidae, even though it is smaller and lighter than the cockroaches we usually associate with this family (e.g. *Blaberus*, *Byrsotria*).

Exercise—**5.3**—RESPIRATION AND METABOLISM

Respiration literally means breathing, but in modern biology it refers specifically to the role of oxygen in extracting energy from the breakdown of sugars. Breathing is referred to as ventilation, the process of pumping air into and out of the body. Oxygen, which is transported to the cells of the body for respiration, is exchanged for carbon dioxide, which is the product of respiration. Metabolism is the sum total of all of the chemical processes that occcur in the body, including the breakdown of nutritional molecules, extraction of energy from this breakdown, and the synthesis of new molecules for growth, development and maintenance. The rate of metabolism is often <u>estimated</u> by measuring the rate of oxygen consumption by an organism or a sample of tissue, as nearly all metabolic processes require oxygen. In the following experiments we will concentrate on investigations of ventilatory movements and metabolic rate of cockroaches. Several variables for these experiments are suggested, but your imagination should yield a few more.

A. <u>VENTILATORY MOVEMENTS AND SPIRACULAR OPENING</u>. As with rate of heartbeat, we might expect to find regulation of pumping air into the tracheal system. We can assess the regulatory abilities of cockroaches by recording the pumping actions of the abdominal muscles (ventilatory movements) and the opening and closing of the spiracular valves. These actions are analogous to breathing in mammals.

(1) <u>Observations of ventilatory movements</u>. The simplest way to observe ventilatory movements is to anesthetize cockroaches with carbon dioxide (from a tank of compressed gas or from dry ice held over the insects). As the cockroaches go under anesthesia they will pump their abdomens vigorously and the spiracles will open as wide as possible. This experiment, however, does not allow sufficient time to quantitatively record the rate of abdominal pumping or the opening of the spiracles. You have to provide carbon dioxide to the cockroaches in low concentrations in order to observe changes in ventilation that can be measured.

First, record the ventilatory movements of resting cockroaches to gather base line data, as with rate of heartbeat. Record the values obtained in DATA BLANK I. Then, if possible, flood the container holding the cockroach with 5%, 10% or 15% carbon dioxide. Mixtures of gases can be prepared using the graduated cylinder technique of Welsh and Smith (1960) (see Methods section). A somewhat less accurate method is to add pure carbon dioxide to the container for a few seconds. You can also inject cockroaches (see BOX #3) with carbon dioxide-saline, prepared as in Exercise 5.2.D(4). Record abdominal pumping and the spiracular openings, and then repeat the experiments with a second group of cockroaches.

Another variable you can test is the effect of heat and cold on ventilatory movements. Place the cockroach in a dish which is inside a larger dish filled with water or a controlled temperature water bath). Change the temperature of the water from room temperature to 10° higher, and record ventilatory movements. Repeat, using ice water to lower the temperature. In nature, what affect would temperature changes have on metabolic rate of cockroaches?

==

DATA BLANK I. Ventilatory movements and spiracular opening/closing

Experiment	Average ventilatory movements (pumps per min)	Spiracles	
		Open	Closed
Resting cockroach			
Stressed cockroach			
CO_2-treatment			
Heat °C			
°C			
°C			
Cold °C			
°C			
°C			
Other variables:			

==

NOTES:

(1) You will have to decide what criteria to use for 'open' and 'closed' spiracles. For example, you could use a range from 1 to 5, 1 being totally closed, and 5 being totally open.

(2) Use the t-test or the Mann-Whitney U-test to compare averages between experiments (see Appendix I).

(2) <u>Control</u> of <u>spiracular valves</u>. Does carbon dioxide affect the spiracular valves locally or indirectly through a central carbon dioxide sensor somewhere else in the body? To answer this question, dissect out the integument that supports one of the thoracic spiracles. Place the tissue on a microscope slide in a dish. Focus on the spiracular opening, and fill the dish with carbon dioxide. Does the spiracle open independently of influences from the rest of the body?

B. <u>RESPIRATION</u>. To measure the utilization of oxygen by a cockroach it is necessary to measure the loss of oxygen from the air inside of a vessel that contains the cockroach. This can be accomplished in a variety of ways using simple or sophistocated instrumentation. All such devices are called respirometers, and most work on the principle that the air pressure in a closed vessel will be reduced when oxygen is removed from the air. Changes in air pressure can easily be measured with a barometer. If a Gilson-type of respirometer or Scholander plexiglas respirometers are available, use one of these instruments according to the accompanying instructions (or see Scholander, 1950). Briefly, the animal is placed in a vessel containing a carbon dioxide-absorbent such as KOH; the loss of oxygen is measured directly on a calibrated pipette or by manipulating a syringe or micrometer.

A simple respirometer can be devised by inserting a 1 ml pipette through a 1-hole rubber stopper and into a glass bottle (Fig. 5.2). The glass bottle must contain a piece of rolled up filter paper previously soaked in 15% KOH, and isolated from the animal (that will also go into the bottle) by several layers of screen. Place the respirometers horizontally on a rack in a water bath (all at the same temperature and all at the same time), so that the tips of the pipettes are immersed below the surface of the water. As oxygen is removed from the air by the cockroach in the bottle, water will enter the pipette. Record the volume of water entering the pipettes every 15 min. to determine the amount of oxygen consumed (in mm³ of oxygen). Readings during the first 20 min or so will probably be erratic, as the respirometers equilibrate. If problems are encountered with one or more respirometers, check for air leakage.

Using one of the techniques listed above, determine the respiratory rate of cockroaches. The following variables might be considered in planning your experiments. (1) temperature (does the respiratory rate double if you double the temperature?), (2) weight of cockroaches (does a small cockroach respire more per gram of body weight than does a larger cockroach?), (3) females producing egg cases <u>vs</u> those that are not, (4) males <u>vs</u> females. Record your data in DATA BLANK II.

<u>METHODS</u>

<u>The Preparation of Gas Mixtures</u>. The making up of mixtures of nitrogen, oxygen, and carbon dioxide in desired proportions for use in experiments on respiratory control is often necessary. This may be accomplished most conveniently by the use of a graduated spirometer such as is commonly used in courses on vertebrate physiology. The gases to be mixed, or added to air, must be obtained in commercially-available cylinders equipped with proper outlet valves. If a spirometer is unavailable, the simple gadget illustrated in Fig. 5.3 is satisfactory for experiments in which the gas mixtures do not have to be exact. The apparatus is constructed from a large graduated cylinder (2000 ml. is convenient), cut off just below the spout and plugged with a large rubber stopper. It should be set near a sink to provide for overflow. The steps in its operation in making up

==

DATA BLANK II. Respirometry

Experimental variables	mm^3 O_2 per hour per gram weight

==

NOTES:

Calculate respiratory rate (mm^3 O_2 per hour) for individual cockroaches. You will find, as might be expected, that larger individuals consume more oxygen than smaller individuals. But, when you divide the rate values by the weights of the cockroaches, is there a significant difference between large and small individuals in rate per gram body weight? Ask your instructor if a shrew and an elephant have similar respiratory rates per gram body weight.

(e.g.) a mixture of 10% oxygen and 90% nitrogen are as follows:

1. Set overflow reservoir at or above top of cylinder. Connect water-inlet tube to tap.
2. Open pinchcocks 1 and 2, and admit water until it fills graduate and overflows both the overflow and gas tubes, displacing all air.
3. Close pinchcock 1. Shut off water.
4. Lower overflow reservoir to desired level of first component of gas mixture to be added (in this case to 10%, as shown in Fig. 5.3).
5. Attach oxygen cylinder to gas tube, open pinchcock 1, and slowly admit oxygen, displacing water to 10% mark.
6. Shut off gas, close pinchcock 1, disconnect gas tube from oxygen cylinder.
7. Lower overflow reservoir to next desired level (in this case to 100%).
8. Connect nitrogen cylinder to gas tube, open pinchcock 1, and slowly admit nitrogen, displacing water to 100% mark.
9. Shut off gas, close pinchcock 1, disconnect gas tube from nitrogen cylinder.
10. Close pinchcock 2.
11. Connect gas tube to experimental vessel, animal chamber, etc.
12. Open pinchcock 1, turn on water, and <u>slowly</u> displace gas mixture into experimental vessel.

<u>Notes</u>: a) Commercial gas cylinders may carry pressures as high as 2000 pounds per square inch. <u>Handle</u> <u>with</u> <u>great</u> <u>care</u>. Do not cement the rubber stopper into the gas-collecting graduate, so that in case of a mistake the stopper is forced out, causing only a moderate spilling of water. <u>Never</u> <u>allow</u> <u>oil</u> <u>to</u> <u>come</u> <u>in</u> <u>contact</u> <u>with</u> <u>oxygen</u> <u>valves</u>. b) The solubility of gases in water may cause some inexactness in the final mixture, expecially when carbon dioxide is used. It is simpler to allow this, since no method is entirely exact, and one can analyze the gas mixture if it seems desirable to check the concentrations of oxygen and carbon dioxide used. (<u>Preparation</u> <u>of</u> <u>Gas</u> <u>Mixtures</u> from Welsh and Smith, 1960, <u>Invertebrate</u> <u>Physiology</u>).

MATERIALS

Cockroaches (different sizes, sexes, species)
Dissecting microscope and instruments
Source of CO_2

Water bath (or temperature-control device)
Ice cubes
Respirometers
Stop watch

NOTES TO INSTRUCTOR

1. Carbon dioxide-air mixtures may be employed, rather than carbon dioxide-oxygen mixtures for ventilation experiments. Simply fill the spirometer with 90% air and then displace the remaining volume with compressed carbon dioxide gas for a 10% carbon dioxide mixture.
2. Stanbury (1968) offers another home-made respirometer which may be used instead of the bottle respirometer. The bottle method is quite adequate for qualitative measurements of respiratory rates, but inaccuracies are easily introduced by temperature fluctuations, leakage and problems such as pipettes being oriented differently.
3. An experiment that might be considered for advanced students is the effects of hormones and stress on blood sugar (trehalose) concentration (see Downer, 1979, 1981).

Fig. 5.2. A simple type of respirometer constructed from a glass bottle, rubber stopper and a pipette.

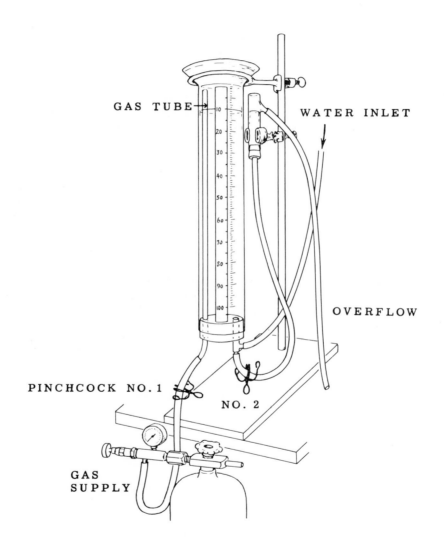

Fig. 5.3. Apparatus for preparing gas mixtures constructed from a graduated cylinder.

GENERAL READINGS

Chippendale, G.M. 1978. The functions of carbohydrates in insect life processes. In: Biochemistry of Insects, Ed. by M. Rockstein. New York: Academic Press.

Downer, R.G.H. 1979. Induction of hypertrehalosemia by excitation in Periplaneta Americana. J. Ins. Physiol. 25:59-63.

Downer, R.G.H. 1981. Fat body and metabolism. In: The American Cockroach, Ed. by W.J. Bell and K.G. Adiyodi. London: Chapman & Hall.

Keeley, L.L. 1978. Endocrine regulation of fat body development and function. Annu. Rev. Entomol. 23:329-352.

Miller, P.L. 1974. Respiration - Aerial gas transport. In: Physiology of Insecta, vol. 6, Ed. by M. Rockstein. New York: Academic Press.

Miller, P.L. 1981. Respiration. In: The American Cockroach, Ed. by W.J. Bell and K.G. Adiyodi. London: Chapman & Hall.

Scholander, P.F. 1950. Volumetric plastic respirometers. Rev. Sci. Instr. 21:378-380.

Stanbury, P. 1968. In: Experiments in Physiology and Biochemistry, Vol. 1, Ed. by G. A. Kerkut. New York: Academic Press.

Welsh, J. H. and Smith, R. I. 1960. Laboratory Exercises in Invertebrate Physiology, Section II. Minneapolis: Burgess Publ. Co.

RESEARCH REPORTS

Baudet, J.L. and Dellier, E. 1975. Recherches sur l'appareil respiratoire des Blattes. II. Les vésiculations trachéenes et leur évolution dans le sous-ordre de Blattaria. Ann. Soc. Entomol. France 11:481-489.

Dehnel, P.A. and Segal, E. 1956. Acclimation of oxygen-consumption to temperature in the American cockroach Periplaneta americana. Biol. Bull. (Wood's Hole) 111:53-61.

Richards, A.G. 1963. The effect of temperature on the rate of oxygen consumption and on the oxidative enzymes in the cockroach, Periplaneta americana. Ann. Entomol. Soc. Amer. 56:355-357.

Scholander, P.F., Flagg, W., Walters, F. and Irving, L. 1953. Climatic adaptation in arctic and tropical poikilotherms. Physiol. Zool. 26:67-92.

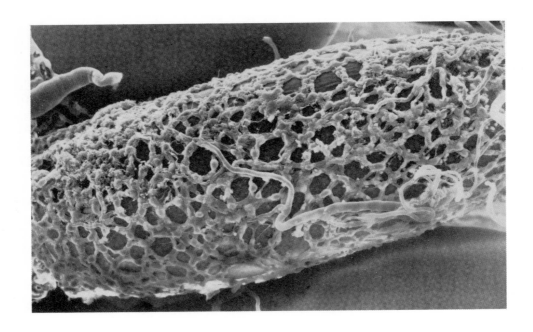

Scanning electron micrograph of the ovarian surface illustrating the cellular sheath.

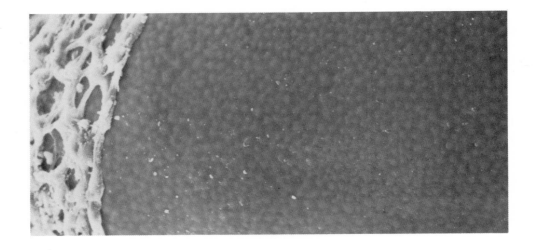

Enlargement of the surface of one follicle. Each round spot is a follicle cell, many of which compose the follicular epithelium that encloses the oocyte.

Exercise-5.4—REPRODUCTION: CONTROL MECHANISMS

Cockroach reproduction illustrates several interesting physiological concepts that are relatively difficult to show with higher animals. First, there are at least three types of reproductive mechanisms among cockroaches. Oviparous females hold the ootheca outside of the body. Ovoviviparous species retract the ootheca into the uterus, where egg development occurs. A few species are pseudoviviparous, with small nutritive cords supplying some of the nutrients to growing embryos. Second, reproduction is under hormonal control, and a feedback mechanism regulates the reproductive cycle in some species.

The following experimental guide emphasizes methods to delineate a reproductive cycle and ways to explore feedback control mechanisms. To perform all of the experiments, representatives of the Blattidae (Periplaneta or Blatta), Blattellidae (Blattella) and the Blaberidae (Blaberus, Leucophaea, or Nauphoeta) are required.

A. REPRODUCTIVE CYCLES. To chart a reproductive cycle it is necessary to collect data from individuals, either by marking or isolating females. Marking is best, as the individuals can be allowed to inhabit cages with males and other females. (Refer to Box #4 for details on how to mark cockroaches). The best species to start with is one of the Blattids or Blattellids; their oothecae remain external, and if you miss oviposition on Sunday you can still observe the ootheca on Monday. With the Blaberids, the ootheca is formed externally, but it is then retracted into the uterus and cannot be observed externally. To see if a Blaberid is 'pregnant,' gently open the last abdominal terga with blunt forceps - the posterior end of the ootheca can easily be observed.

Each day every marked female should be checked to record reproductive condition: ovulation and oviposition (ootheca being formed) (Fig. 5.4), 'pregnancy' (holding an ootheca externally or internally), or no observable signs of reproduction. Set one stage, such as 'ootheca forming', as the first day of the reproductive cycle and plot the cycle on DATA BLANK II for several females until another ootheca forms. Once a cycle is determined, as shown for Blattella germanica (Fig. 5.5), the next step is to dissect females on each day during the cycle to better understand the internal physiological changes. Measure the length of developing eggs (as shown in Fig. 5.5) and record changes in the colleterial glands or other parts of the reproductive system. Further experiments might include the effect of food or water deprivation, stress from crowding or isolation from other cockroaches.

B. CONTROL OF REPRODUCTION. Researchers have shown that reproduction (yolk deposition) in cockroaches is stimulated by juvenile hormone secreted by the corpora allata (an endocrine gland in the head). To duplicate experiments that confirm this theory in Blattids, tie a tight ligature (of thread) around the posterior part of the neck of 2-or 3-day old virgin newly-emerged females. Keep the ligatured females in a humid incubator to avoid desiccation. To some of these females apply 1 µg of juvenile hormone in acetone to the dorsal cuticle. To the others, apply acetone only. As acetone is poisonous, it is essential to apply as little of this solvent as possible; 1 µl is optimal. Dissect the females after 12 to 14 days and compare egg development in hormone-treated and control females.

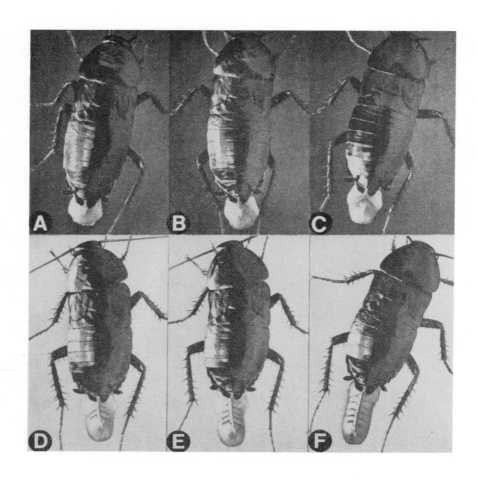

Fig. 5.4. Oviposition and ootheca formation in Blatta orientalis. Time course: A, 0-hr; B, 1-hr; C, 2-hr; D, 4-hr; E, 5-hr; F, 8-hr (ootheca nearly complete).

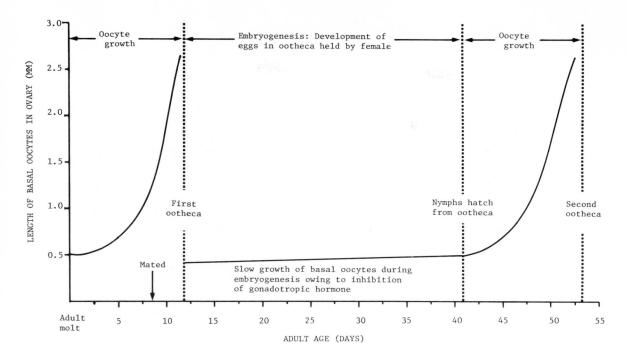

Fig. 5.5. Oocyte (egg) growth and ootheca formation in Blattella germanica after the adult molt. Between the two periods of oocyte growth, the embryos are incubated in the ootheca held by the female.

BOX-4

MARKING COCKROACHES. Any kind of paper disk with a number, letter, or color code can be used to mark individual cockroaches. Coat the disk with Scotch spraymount adhesive while holding it with forceps over newspaper. Apply slight pressure for 10 seconds after placing the disk on the pronotum. More permanent markings can be made by rubbing the cuticle with a small amount of acetone, touching on a dot of 'super glue,' and then painting the super glue with enamel.

===

DATA BLANK I. Hypothetical reproductive cycle plotted according to
              ootheca formation

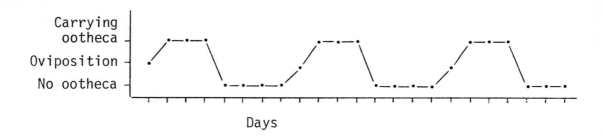

Days

===

DATA BLANK II. Reproductive cycle of _____ _____

Days

Reproductive cycle of _____ _____

Days

Reproductive cycle of _____ _____

Days

===

Similar experiments with the same results can be achieved with Blaberids or Blattellids, but with these species a different experiment can also be performed to demonstrate a feedback system. The first step is to remove the ootheca from the uterus of several pregnant females. As a result the females will initiate development of another batch of eggs that would not have developed in the pregnant female. These observations suggest that the neuroendocrine system receives information from the uterus or ootheca relating the pregnancy state of the female. Owing to these signals, hormones that stimulate egg development are not secreted; after the eggs hatch the negative feedback information is curtailed and the hormones for egg development are once again secreted. This scheme is diagrammed in Fig. 5.6.

Two interesting experiments can be conducted regarding the feedback system. First, when the ventral nerve cord of a pregnant female is severed (by a hooked pin inserted through an intersegmental membrane), egg development begins in the ovaries, even though an ootheca is present in the uterus. Secondly, inserting tiny glass beads (~ 4 mm diameter) into the uterus of a pregnant female from which the ootheca was removed, prevents egg development in the ovaries; in other words the neuroendocrine system continues to receive 'pregnancy signals.' Students should be able to determine the significance of these experiments; if not, the references may be consulted.

C. OOTHECA FORMATION. How do cockroach eggs become lined up in 2 parallel rows, coated with the ootheca material and formed into the sculptured egg container called an ootheca? To answer this question, secure an ovulating female with modeling clay under a binocular microscope and watch carefully as each egg is ovulated and manipulated. By partially dissecting the female, and adding saline, both the inside and outside actions can be observed simultaneously. Interesting biochemical experiments can also be formulated concerning hardening and darkening of material secreted by the colleterial glands (see reference by Brunet, 1951).

D. PARTHENOGENESIS. Virgin Periplaneta americana females used in behavioral experiments will produce egg cases and, if these are protected from munching parents, will hatch live nymphs. Are these nymphs healthy and normal? Will they all be females? If they are females can they also reproduce without being fertilized?

MATERIALS

Juvenile hormone (see Appendix II for suppliers)
Acetone
Glass beads
Thread for ligatures

Dissecting microscope, dissecting dish and instruments
Modeling clay
Female Blattidae (Periplaneta) and Blaberidae (Blaberus or Leucophaea)

NOTES TO INSTRUCTOR

1. Students may construct reproductive cycles based on external (ootheca) and/or internal (eggs) measurements.
2. Females will not mate during the first 8 days after the adult molt, and so you do not necessarily have to pick out newly molted females to insure virginity.

GENERAL READINGS

Bell, W. J. and Adiyodi, K. G. 1981. Reproduction. In: The American Cockroach, Ed. by W. J. Bell and K. G. Adiyodi. London: Chapman and Hall.

Doane, W. 1973. Role of hormones in insect development. In: Developmental Systems: Insects, Vol. 2, Ed. by S. J. Counce and C. H. Waddington. New York: Academic Press.

Engelmann, F. 1970. The Physiology of Insect Reproduction. New York: Pergamon Press.

Riddiford, L. M. 1980. Insect Endocrinology: Action of hormones at the cellular level. Annu. Rev. Physiol. 42: 511-528.

Roth, L. M. 1970. Evolution and taxonomic significance of reproduction in Blattaria. Annu. Rev. Entomol. 15: 75-96.

Tobe, S. S. 1980. Regulation of the corpora allata in adult female insects. In: Insect Biology in the Future, Ed. by M. Locke and D. S. Smith. New York: Academic Press.

Tobe, S. S. and Stay, B. 1981. Endocrines. In: The American Cockroach, Ed. by W. J. Bell and K. G. Adiyodi. London: Chapman & Hall.

RESEARCH REPORTS

Anderson, E. 1964. Oocyte differentiation and vitellogenesis in the roach Periplaneta americana. J. Cell Biol. 20: 131-155.

Bell, W. J. 1969a. Dual role of juvenile hormone in the control of yolk formation in Periplaneta americana. J. Insect Physiol. 15: 1270-1290.

Bell, W. J. 1969b. Continuous and rhythmic reproductive cycle observed in Periplaneta americana L. Biol. Bull. (Woods Hole) 137: 239-249.

Bonhag, P. F. 1959. Histological and histochemical studies on the ovary of the American cockroach Periplaneta americana (L.). Univ. Calif. Publ. Entomol. 16: 81-124.

Brunet, P. C. J. 1951. The formation of the ootheca by Periplaneta americana. I. The micro-anatomy and histology of the posterior part of the abdomen. Quart. Micr. Sci. 92: 113-127.

Mullins, D. E. and C. B. Keil. 1980. Paternal investment of urates in cockroaches. Nature (Lond.) 283: 567-569.

Fig. 5.6. Feedback control of the reproductive cycle of Blaberids and some Blattellids. The brain stimulates the corpus allatum (CA) to secrete juvenile hormone (jh) which induces yolk deposition in the oocytes of the ovary. Mature eggs are ovulated, oviposited into an ootheca and withdrawn into the uterus. Stretch receptors in the uterus transmit signals via the central nervous system to inhibit the brain from stimulating the CA. jh secretion ceases and yolk deposition stops. After the nymphs hatch from the ootheca, the cycle begins again. Compare this diagram with the events shown in Fig. 5.5.

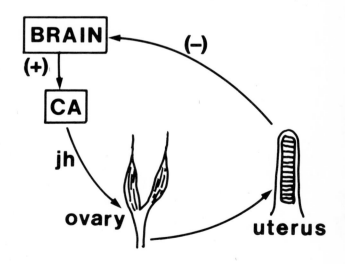

Exercise—**5.5**—EMBRYOGENESIS: DEVELOPMENT WITHIN THE EGG CASE

Eggs of cockroaches are relatively large (up to 9 mm in length) and yolky. Each egg is bounded by two membranes, an inner vitelline membrane and a tough shell or chorion. The chorion has tiny holes that allow gaseous exchange and larger holes, micropyles, that permit entry of sperm cells during fertilization.

Embryogenesis is the process by which the egg divides into many small cells which then migrate and specialize to form an embryo. Insects differ from most other animals in that the fertilized egg does not actually divide sequentially into many smaller cells. The nucleus divides, and then the daughter nuclei divide and so on until a large number of nuclei are produced. These migrate to the periphery and become enclosed by cell membranes. Thus the end result is the same as in other animals, but the mechanism for achieving the product is different. The cockroach embryo, comprised of many small cells, grows around the yolk, and at the same time groups of cells form the organs of the body. As with embryos of other animals, the embryonic cells first sort out into three types of tissues: ectoderm, mesoderm and endoderm. Figures 5.7 and 5.8 further explain the processes of embryogenesis in cockroaches.

A. OBSERVING LIVING EMBRYOS. Two problems must be overcome before an embryo can be observed. These are removing embryos from the ootheca without injuring them and maintaining embryos outside the ootheca for relatively long time periods. These problems have recently been solved by a researcher studying the behavior of embryos (Provine, 1976, 1977, 1981). First, sterilize the ootheca by sequentially dipping it in solutions of 2% iodine, 95% ethyl alcohol and sterile distilled water. Second, remove chorionated embryos from the ootheca; Periplaneta, Blatta, Blattella and Parcoblatta work best. Crack open the ootheca carefully along the crimped edge. Remove the embryos, place them on a moistened filter paper on the floor of a Petri dish and put on the cover. Keep the filter paper moist, but not wet, with drops of sterile distilled water. Put the dishes in a larger container such as a desiccator jar containing wet cotton to maintain humid conditions. The best temperature for maintaining embryos is 29° C. To view embryos at various stages, place them in 3% hypochlorite solution (Bentley et al., 1979) for a few minutes to dissolve the opaque chorion.

To investigate Blaberid embryos it is necessary to record the time after pregnant females oviposit (see Exercise 5.4). Refer to Table 5.2 to determine when to remove the ootheca from the uterus for setting up these embryos in culture.

B. STAGING EMBRYOS. Table 5.2 provides information on the general development times for cockroach eggs and Table 5.1 provides complete data for Blattella germanica. Since most of the dynamic changes occur in the last one-third of the development period, oothecae may be held until that time. Remember that development proceeds more slowly below 26° C., and faster at higher temperatures.

C. EMBRYONIC DEVELOPMENT. Most developing systems must be studied by embedding embryos in paraffin and making thin sections for viewing under a compound microscope (see Provine, 1981; Counce, 1973; Johannsen and Butt, 1941). The following aspects of development are those that can be readily observed using whole embryos or partially dissected embryos. A

69

Table 5.1. Descriptions of lateral view and outer view stages of
    Blattella germanica embryos.

Days at 25° C	Stage in Figure 5.7	Lateral view stages of embryos
0-2	1	Only yolk granules observable
3	2	Germ band slightly expanded at both ends
4$^-$	3	Rudiments of head and thoracic appendages appear
4$^+$	4	Abdominal segmentation appears; tail begins to fold
5	5	Segmentation of abdomen completed; tail folded
6	6	Yolk becomes uneven; antennae and legs grow posteriorly
7	7	Segmentation of legs occurs
8	8	Caudal space arises
9$^-$	9	Amnion and serosa rupture; dorsal organ formed; embryo shifts downward; legs folded
9$^+$	10	Embryo grows rapidly
10	11	Dorsal closure of body wall
12	12	Eye coloration begins; tips of antennae and hind legs reach 3rd abdominal segment (a.s.)
14	13	Eye color distinct; tips of antennae reach 4th a.s.
16	14	Tips of antennae reach 4th a.s.
18	15	Tips of antennae reach 5th a.s.
20	16	Mandible coloration; tips of antennae reach 6th a.s.
22	17	Bristles observable; tips of antennae reach 7th a.s.
24	18	Bristles conspicuous; tips of antennae reach 8th a.s.

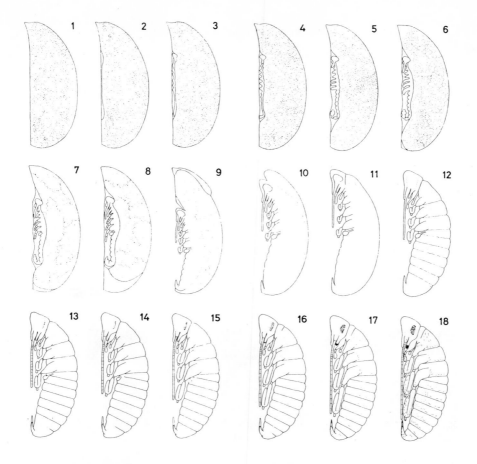

Fig. 5.7. Visual stages of embryogenesis in <u>Blattella germanica</u>. Refer to Table 5.1 for descriptions of embryological development.

Fig. 5.8. The cockroach embryo begins as a '<u>germ band</u>', growing on the surface of the <u>yolk</u> within an envelope of two membranes, the <u>serosa</u> and <u>amnion</u>. Growth proceeds laterally, with the embryo eventually surrounding the yolk. At one point the tail end pushes into the yolk to increase the absorptive surface for uptake of the yolk nutrients. Internal organs develop at the same time that external structures appear. The final stage is dorsal closure, when the lateral margins of the embryo meet at the dorsal midline. Before hatching, the yolk material has been completely utilized to build a cockroach nymph. h, head lobe; s, serosa; y, yolk; a, amnion.

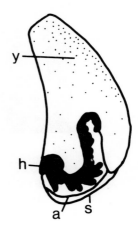

71

Table 5.2. Approximate time periods for embryonic development

Species	Dates
Periplaneta americana	40-49
Periplaneta australasiae	40-49
Blatta orientalis	45-56
Eurycotis floridana	47-55
Supella longipalpa	40-50
Blattella germanica	20-35
Leucophaea maderae	58-84
Nauphoeta cinerea	30-40

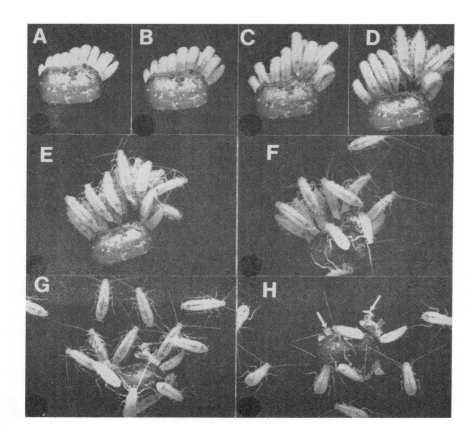

Fig. 5.9. Nymphs of Periplaneta americana hatching in unison from an ootheca. Arrows in (H) show embryonic cuticle that is shed prior to hatching. (A-G) taken at 1 minute intervals; (H) taken 20-minutes after (A).

dissecting microscrope and careful technique are required.

(1) <u>Development of cuticular structures</u>.   Even   if   culturing   is   not attempted, one can open oothecae of different ages, remove the chorion and observe the embryos (Fig. 5.7).   Either drawings or photographs can be used to record developmental sequences.   Of interest is the formation of legs, antennae and segmentation of the body.   Preserve embryos in 95% ethyl alcohol for later investigation.

(2) <u>Internal organs</u>.   Dissect embryos with watchmaker's forceps and pins. In older embryos it is possible to observe the digestive tract as it forms around the remaining yolk.   Reproductive organs remain very small even in nymphs.   The ventral nerve cord can sometimes be observed.

(3) <u>Heart and circulation</u>.   In young embryos the heart appears as a motionless tube.   At a certain stage, however, the heart begins to pulse in all 16 embryos (no dissection is necessary).   The embryos appear to be 'alive' when the heart begins to beat.

(4) <u>Embryonic behavior</u>.   <u>Periplaneta</u> <u>americana</u> embryos begin to twitch on about day 16 or 17, and powerful hatching movements occur on about day 30.   The timing of these movements seems to be controlled by an internal clock.   Hatching involves shedding of the embryonic cuticle and synchronized pushing open of the ootheca by all 16 the nymphs. If some littermates cannot participate in hatching because of death or weakness or asynchronized development, all of the inhabitants of the ootheca 'will be trapped in the ootheca and die' (Provine, 1981).

(5) <u>Hatching</u>.   Maintain some of the oothecae intact so that hatching can be observed.   Removing oothecae from Blaberids during the final week of incubation in the uterus will often initiate hatching of these embryos.   Fig. 5.9 illustrates nymphs hatching from an ootheca.

MATERIALS

Dissecting microscope (with camera if available); dissecting dish and instruments

Oothecae of <u>Periplaneta</u>, <u>Blatta</u> or <u>Blattella</u> and pregnant female <u>Blaberus</u> or <u>Leucophaea</u>

Petri dishes (plastic or glass)

Filter paper

3% Hypochlorite solution

Sterile distilled water (either autoclaved or boiled for 10 min)

2% Iodine solution (2 g Iodine, 100 ml distilled water)

95% Ethyl alcohol

Desiccator jar or similar container

NOTES TO INSTRUCTOR

1. Working with 5 mm and 8 mm long embryos is difficult and requires practice.   Observations of staged embryos, on the other hand, can be managed by students of all ages.   The time periods listed in Table 5.2 are only estimates, owing to the influence of environmental conditions.
2. Students should be encouraged to use the information gathered in Exercise 5.4 to determine pregnancy periods of female cockroaches.   The time periods listed in Table 5.2 are only estimates owing to the influence of environmental conditions.

3. Internal anatomy of embryos must be studied to completely understand embryogenesis. Students should be referred to the GENERAL READINGS and perhaps a general embryology text.

GENERAL READINGS

Counce, S. J. 1973. The causal analysis of insect embryogenesis. In: Developmental Systems: Insects, Vol. 2, Ed. by S. J. Counce and C. H. Waddington. New York: Academic Press.

Johannsen, O. A. and F. H. Butt. 1941. Embryology of Insects and Myriapods. New York: McGraw-Hill.

Bodenstein, D. 1953. Postembryonic development. In: Insect Physiology, Ch. 30, Ed. by K. D. Roeder. New York: Wiley.

Bodenstein, D. 1955. Insects. In: Analysis of Development, Ed. by B. Willier, P. Weiss and V. Hamburger. New York: Saunders.

Provine, R. R. 1976 . Development of function in nerve nets. In: Simpler Networks and Behavior, Ch. 14, Ed. by J. Fentress. Sunderland, Mass.: Sinauer Associates.

Provine, R. R. Embryogenesis and development. In: The American Cockroach, Ed. by W. J. Bell and K. G. Adiyodi. London: Chapman & Hall.

RESEARCH REPORTS

Bentley, D., Keshishian, H., Shankland, M and Toroian-Raymond, A. 1979. Quantitative staging of embryonic development of the grasshopper, Schistocerca niten. J. Embryol. exp. Morph. 54:47-74.

Chen, J. S. and R. Levi-Montalcini. 1969. Axonal outgrowth and cell migration in vitro from nervous system of cockroach embyros. Science 166: 631-632.

Provine, R. R. 1976. Eclosion and hatching in cockroach first instar larvae: A stereotyped pattern of behavior. J. Insect Physiol. 22: 127-131.

Sanders, K. 1976. Specification of the basic body pattern in insect embryogenesis. Adv. Insect Physiol. 12: 125-238.

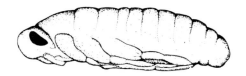

Exercise — 5.6 — REGENERATION: RESTORATION OF LOST PARTS

When a cockroach nymph loses a leg or antenna it is capable of regenerating a new one. The adaptive nature of this ability becomes obvious if you inspect the nymphs in your colony and note that many individuals are missing one or more appendages. If you have attempted to catch one of these cockroaches you will also see that legs pull off quite easily (better a leg than a life).

In order for tissues (epidermis, muscle, nerves) to regenerate, they must go through a series of stages in which the wound is healed and then the existing tissues replicate the lost part. The major question addressed in the experiments in this chapter is how do the remaining tissues "know" the type and size of structures that need to be restored.

Formation of new structures can only occur during periods between molts (see Exercise 5.7), and completely or nearly completely regenerated structures appear after a molt.

Experiments with regeneration of legs and other structures have potential for increasing our understanding of animal development. In a way, regeneration represents the re-stimulation of embryogenesis, a capability that is peculiar to only a few parts of some organisms. After completing the experiments in this chapter, consider the relationships between regeneration and embryogenesis.

A. HOW MANY COCKROACHES HAVE LOST LEGS? It is possible to answer this question, for example, with Periplaneta americana trapped in an infested area, by counting the tarsal segments on each leg (see Fig. 4.4): a normal (original?) tarsus has 5 segments, and a regenerated one has 4.

B. ARE REGENERATED LEGS AS LONG AS NORMAL LEGS? Obtain cockroach nymphs that have recently molted (within 2 to 5 days), and cut off one leg from each animal. As an option, remove the legs at different joints and record this information for each marked animal (see Box #4). After the next molt, measure the new leg and the leg on the opposite side of the animal. Are they equal in length? Suppose you allow 2 or 3 molts to occur--any changes?

C. HOW DOES A STUMP KNOW THAT THE REST OF THE LEG IS MISSING? Several hypotheses seem worth considering: (1) wounding alone stimulates the remaining structures to produce a new leg; (2) factors are produced at the wound site that stimulate regeneration of a new leg; (3) information continually flows up the leg, inhibiting regeneration; when the flow of information ceases, a new leg is produced, (4) others?

To determine if any one of these hypotheses is valid, perform the following experiments. Cut a notch in the tibia of a cockroach nymph as shown in Fig. 5.10. Replace the notch and seal it (as described in the Methods) in some of the animals and leave the wound open in the other animals. Do the results, after the animals molt, suggest which of the hypotheses may be most correct?

Next, cut both left and right mesothoracic tibiae at the half-way point and swap the amputated portions as shown in Fig. 5.11A. Be sure to fix the grafted legs in the same position as before they were cut (ventral-dorsal axes must be the same, but the anterior-posterior axes will

Fig. 5.10. Cutting a deep notch in the tibia of a cockroach results in the growth of a tarsus at the point of incision. Why a tarsus and not another tibia?

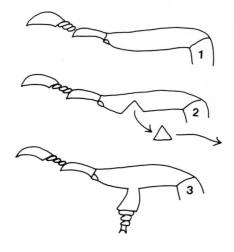

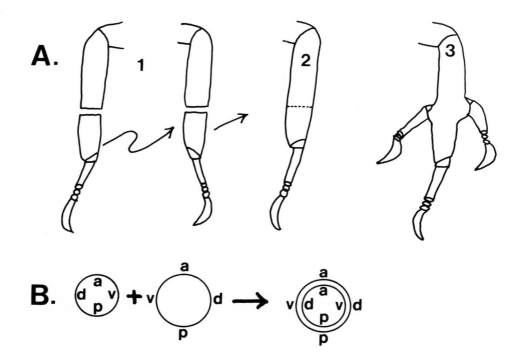

Fig. 5.11. (A) Graft of the left to right mesothoracic tibia; after the cockroach molts, two tarsi grow from the point of graft attachment. (B) Diagram indicating how to interpret the results (see also, Bohn, 1965).

be different). Seal the grafts and wait until the nymph has molted. How do you explain the results? Fig. 5.11B may aid your interpretation. A similar experiment which may be easier, is to cut one tibia, turn it 180 degrees, and seal it back on. The result should be similar to that in the last experiment.

D. HOW DOES A STUMP KNOW WHAT PART OF THE LEG TO PRODUCE?
Obviously if a femur stump produced a tarsus, the regenerated leg would not be very useful. The femur stump 'knows,' therefore, to produce the rest of the femur, a tibia and then a tarsus. The tibia stump should complete a tibia and also produce a new tarsus. What happens when you make the following amputations on different animals: midway through the tibia or femur, or at the junction of the tibia and tarsus. Are the appropriate segments regenerated? Suppose you graft a tarsus to a femur; will the regenerated leg have a tibia?

E. HOW IS LENGTH OF THE REQUIRED REGENERATE DETERMINED BY THE STUMP? Follow the experimental scheme shown in Fig. 5.12A, grafting the two short tibia stumps together and the two long stumps together. Be sure to use two animals, and to graft mesothoracic tibia to mesothoracic tibia, and to position the grafts exactly as in the intact leg. If your results are as expected (Fig. 5.12A), the leg created with two short stumps will generate (after molting) a normal tibia. The two long stumps, however, will generate a 'super' tibia with the spines pointing proximally in the center portion of the regenerate. If you cannot explain these results, Fig. 5.12B provides the necessary clue.

F. DOES THE HOST OR DONER SUPPLY CELLS FOR REGERATED LEGS?
Graft legs, as in any of the experiments above, using two species of cockroaches with different pigmentation. For examples, Periplaneta vs Blatta or Periplaneta vs Blaberus. Are the resulting leg regenerates exactly like the host or donor or a mixture of both?

G. HOW ARE CUTICULAR PATTERNS DETERMINED? Look closely, under a dissecting microscrope, at the pattern of hairs, dents and valleys in the cuticle of the cockroach. Is this pattern determined during embryogenesis? Cut a small square (0.3 cm x 0.3 cm) of integument out of the back of the cockroach (in the abdominal area). Rotate the square by 180° and replace it immediately. Remove excess blood with absorbent tissue and place a small quantity of streptomycin, phenylthiourea and penicillin (in a ratio of 1:2:1) on the wound to inhibit infection. Does the pattern of color, spots or cuticular ridges remain the same after the cockroach molts, or does its appearance change so that it blends into the rest of the terga? This experiment can also be performed using two cockroach species with different pigmentation and/or different cuticular structure.

METHODS

Cutting notches. Anesthetize a cockroach and hold one leg down on a flat surface. Cut a notch using a razor blade or a scalpel.

Sealing grafts. Bohn (1974) uses Nobecutan, 'new skin' (Bastianwerke Müchen) to seal grafts. I have used fingernail polish and collodion with moderate (50%) success, but dental cement (quick drying) works best if you can obtain it. After sealing the graft be sure the sealant is dry before allowing the cockroach to touch surfaces that may adhere to the sealant.

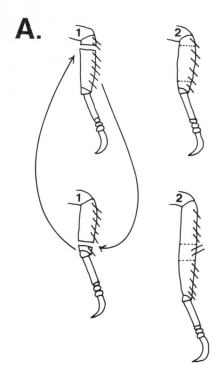

A.

Fig. 5.12. (A) Grafts of short tibia stumps and long tibia stumps result in a normal tibia length in the former case and an exceedingly long tibia in the latter case. (B) Diagram indicating how to interpret the results (see also, Bohn, 1965).

B.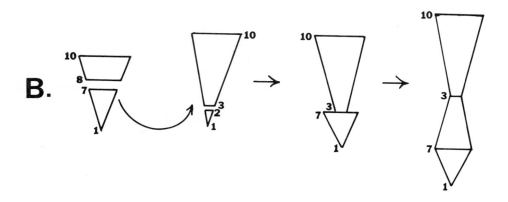

MATERIALS

Cockroaches (nymphs of <u>Leucophaea</u>,
 <u>Blatta</u>, <u>Blaberus</u> and <u>Periplaneta</u>)
Dissecting microscope; dissecting dish
 with wax or cork bottom, and
 dissecting instruments (including
 sharp, fine scissors)
Crystals of streptomycin, penicillin
 and phenylthiourea

Bunsen burner or candle
Graft sealant

NOTES TO INSTRUCTOR

1. Some grafts will be broken off; maintaining graftees in isolation will minimize this problem.
2. Grafting experiments are more difficult than they might seem; regeneration of missing leg parts, on the other hand, is quite easy.
3. Sections C and D-G should be considered as projects, rather than exercises for one laboratory session.

GENERAL READINGS

Bryant, P. J., Bryant, S. V. and V. French. 1977. Biological regeneration and pattern formation. <u>Sci</u>. <u>Amer</u>. 237: 66-81.

Edwards, J. S. and J. Palka. 1976. Neural generation and regeneration in insects. In: <u>Simpler Networks and Behavior</u>, Ed. by J. C. Fentress. Sunderland, Mass.: Sinuer Assoc.

Kunkel, J. 1981. Regeneration. In: <u>The American Cockroach</u>, Ed. by W. J. Bell and K. G. Adiyodi. London: Chapman & Hall.

Lawrence, P. A. 1973. The development of spatial patterns in the integument of insects. In: <u>Developmental Systems</u>: <u>Insects</u>, Vol. 2., Ed. by S. J. counce and C. H. Waddington. New York: Academic Press.

Wolpert, L. 1978. Pattern formation in biological development. <u>Sci</u>. <u>Amer</u>. (Oct.) pp. 154-157.

RESEARCH REPORTS

Bodenstein, D. 1955. Contributions to the problem of regeneration in insects. <u>J</u>. <u>Exp</u>. <u>Zool</u>. 129: 209-224.

Bohn, H. 1965. Analyse der Regenerations fähigkeit der Insektenextremität durch Amputations- und Transplantationsversuche an Larven der afrikanischen Schabe (<u>Leucophaea maderae</u> Fabr.). II. Mitteilung: Achsendetermination. <u>Wilhelm Roux Archiv für Entwicklungsmechanik der Organismen</u> 156: 449-503.

Bohn, H. 1974. Extent and properties of the regeneration field in the larval legs of cockroaches (<u>Leucophaea maderae</u>). I. Extirpation experiments. <u>J</u>. <u>Embryol</u>. <u>Exp</u>. <u>Morphol</u>. 31: 557-572.

Bohn, H. 1976. Tissue interactions in the regenerating cockroach leg. <u>Symp</u>. <u>R</u>. <u>Ent</u>. <u>Soc</u>. 8: 170-185.

French, V. 1976. Leg regeneration in the cockroach, <u>Blattella germanica</u>. II. Regeneration from a non-congruent tibial graft/host junction. <u>J</u>. <u>Embryol</u>. <u>Exp</u>. <u>Morphl</u>. 35: 267-301.

Capucina patula (Blaberidae) lives under bark of rotting trees, and moves out onto the bark at night to feed on lichens and fungi. Adults (winged) and nymphs are cryptically colored to blend into the background (4 individuals are shown in the photo). *Capucina* crouches close to the bark when disturbed.

Exercise – **5.7** – GROWTH AND MOLTING: METAMORPHOSIS

Insects and other arthropods grow in distinct steps rather than gradually as do vertebrates. A cockroach nymph stores the nutrients required for growth, produces a new 'folded' exoskeleton beneath the old one, and then the old exoskeleton is shed during molting. The new exoskeleton stretches out and hardens to provide a larger exoskeleton for the new nymphal stage.

Some insects have a life cycle that involves dramatic changes, from a larva (caterpillar, maggot) to a pupa (resting and developing stage within a cocoon) and an adult (which usually has wings). Such insects are said to have complete metamorphosis. Cockroaches are relatively primitive insects, with incomplete metamorphosis, and the life cycle simply includes increasingly larger nymphs and finally the adult.

A. <u>GROWTH</u>. The growth pattern of cockroaches can be charted in two ways. First and best, you can weigh and measure one group of nymphs after each molt. The molting cycle of a group of nymphs can be regulated by depriving them of food for a few days; then begin feeding them to insure that they will all molt on approximately the same day. Second, you can take a colony of cockroaches, assuming all nymphal stages are represented, and weigh and measure the entire group. Either way you will obtain classes of weights and body sizes. These data might include body length and width, leg length, total body weight, and other indeces that you can think of. We know, for example, that in humans the head is relatively large in babies, whereas legs grow more slowly, and often in spurts. If you measure certain body parts of cockroaches, such as legs, antennae, abdomen or thorax, you can determine if all body parts grow proportionally.

B. <u>CONTROL OF METAMORPHOSIS</u>. Metamorphosis in cockroaches is controlled primarily by three hormones: <u>juvenile hormone</u> (JH), secreted by the corpora allata, <u>ecdysone</u>, secreted by the prothoracic glands, and <u>brain hormone</u> (BH) from neurosecretory cells in the brain. BH stimulates ecdysone secretion which in turn brings about molting. Ecdysone and JH determine if the insect will molt into another nymph or an adult. If JH is present, the product will be a nymph; if JH is absent the product will be an adult.

The following experiment will allow you to prevent a cockroach from becoming an adult--if you persist you can engineer a 'giant' or supernumerary cockroach. JH can be applied in at least two different ways: (1) deposit 10 μg of JH to the cuticle of each cockroach every 3 days, or (2) saturate the filter paper on which the cockroaches walk with 30 mg JH and change the paper every 10 days. Your cockroach will molt normally, but remain 'juvenile.' The most interesting aspect of this experiment is to apply JH to large nymphs that you suspect are ready to become adults. Quite often they molt into super-large nymphs with some adult characteristics. Can these animals reproduce? Calculate the amount of JH that would be required to prevent cockroaches from reaching adulthood in an infested building. How would you apply this knowledge in a biological control program?

C. <u>CUTICULAR TANNING</u>. A cockroach is white immediately after it molts, and then the cuticle becomes darker owing to a tanning process.

Tanning is controlled by a hormone called bursicon, which is produced at a localized region in the cockroach. To determine the approximate site of hormone production, partition the cockroach's body into isolated segments: tie a ligature of thread between the thorax and abdomen, and around the neck of a white, newly molted cockroach. Which part(s) turn dark? Use a syringe to remove a small quantity of blood (100 µl) from the dark segment, and re-inject it into one of the white segments. What happens to the injected segment? What does this indicate about the source of bursicon and the usual means by which this hormone moves throughout the body of the cockroach?

MATERIALS

Juvenile hormone (diluted in olive oil, 10 mg JH:10 ml olive oil; this solution provides 10 µg in a small drop of 10 µl). (See Appendix II for sources of JH)

Filter paper

Balance (mg)
Cm ruler
Pipette (for JH)
Thread (for ligatures)
Micro-syringe (to inject blood)
Capillary tubes (to collect blood)

NOTES TO INSTRUCTOR

1. Ligatures must be tied tightly, but not so that bleeding occurs. Applying haemostats in the bursicon experiments is an alternative to the ligature method.
2. Time required for the bursicon experiment is only a few hours.
3. There are many different kinds of juvenile hormones on the market, and they vary in specificity and potency. You may have to run preliminary experiments to find the appropriate dosage, or refer to a recent publication on the subject.

GENERAL READINGS

Bodenstein, D. 1953. The role of hormones in molting and metamorphosis. In: Insect Physiology. Ed. by K. D. Roeder. New York: Wiley.

Kunkel, J. 1981. Regeneration. In: The American Cockroach, Ed. by W. J. Bell and K. G. Adiyodi. London: Chapman & Hall.

Mills, R. R. 1981. Integument. In: The American Cockroach, Ed. by W. J. Bell and K. G. Adiyodi. London: Chapman & Hall.

RESEARCH REPORTS

Fraenkel, G. and Hsaio, C. 1963. Tanning in the adult fly. Science 141: 1057-1058.

Gier, H. T. 1947. Growth rate in the cockroach Periplaneta americana. Annals Entomol. Soc. Amer. 40:303-317.

Mills, R. R. 1965. Hormonal control of tanning in the American cockroach. II. Assay for the hormone and the effect of wound healing. J. Insect Physiol. 11: 1269-1275.

Exercise-**5.8**—NERVES: CONDUCTION OF SIGNALS

The nervous system is analogous to a telephone system: both consist of cables and both have central control boxes. Signals are generated at one part of the nervous system and carried to other parts; the signals are coded information that stimulate effector organs (such as leg muscles) to respond. The purpose of this exercise is to monitor the signals that are transported in the nervous system.

A. <u>TWO IMPORTANT SENSORY ORGANS</u>. Cockroaches have large compound eyes and probably utilize vision even under low intensity light. Because they are active at night, cockroaches have extremely fine-tuned olfactory (smell) and tactile (touch, vibration, wind current) receptors. A large population of tactile receptors is located on the cerci; you can demonstrate this yourself by blowing puffs of air on cockroaches with and without cerci (remove the cerci with sharp scissors). Prepare the cerci (see Methods section) and examine these organs under a microscope. Each tiny hair on the ventral surface is bent when a puff of wind passes over the circus. Most olfactory receptors are located on the antennae; sensory hairs have pores that allow odorant molecules to contact the membrane of the dendrite part of the nerve cell (see Fig. 4.5). In both cases if the stimulus is great enough, a nerve impulse will be propagated by the sensory cell and transmitted to the central nervous sytem (CNS). This information is processed by the CNS to determine the response of the animal.

B. <u>RECORDING TECHNIQUES</u>. Signals in the nervous system are actually electrical impulses, and can, therefore, be monitored by standard electronic devices that are designed to detect and amplify small changes in voltage. There are basically two simple ways to monitor nerve impulses: viewing the impulse on an oscilloscope and listening to the impulse through a loudspeaker. Two experiments are outlined below for monitoring nerve signals.

(1) <u>Ventral nerve cord preparation</u>. The ventral nerve cord contains very large axons (giant interneurons) that transmit nerve signals to the thoracic ganglion from sensory organs located at the posterior part of the body (Fig. 5.13). In the following experiment we will stimulate the cerci and attempt to 'hear' nerve signals passing up the nerve cord to the thoracic ganglia where motor signals are generated to drive the legs in an escape response (see Exercise 6.5 for more information about the behavioral response).

The following description includes two methods for recording ventral nerve cord signals, one using the amplifier in your hi-fi system (audio amplifier), and the other incorporating a preamplifier between the electrodes and the audio amplifier. In both methods, prepare two hooked, silver wire electrodes soldered to shielded cable (see Methods) and plug the cables into the input jacks of the audio amplifier or preamplifier. if the preamplifier stage is to be used, take the output the preamplifier to the input jacks of the audio amplifier. Amplifiers should be grounded to a water pipe. Hook your speaker up to the back panel of the audio amplifier according to the instructions with the amplifier.

If an oscilloscope is available, connect the output leads from the preamplifier to the oscilloscope, as well as, to the audio amplifier. If you

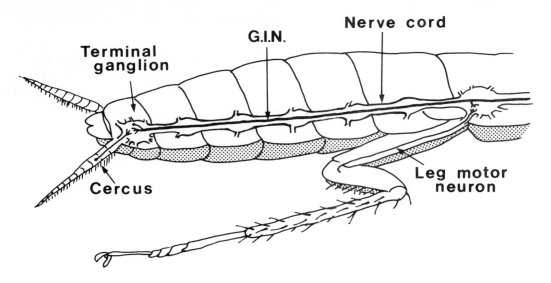

Fig. 5.13. Nerve cells in the cockroach escape system. Nerve impulses generated in wind-receptor neurons in the cerci are transmitted to the terminal ganglion and along giant interneurons (G.I.N.) running up the ventral nerve cord to the metathoracic ganglion. The signals are interpreted within the ganglion to initiate evasive orientation by the cockroach.

Fig. 5.14. Posterior end of a cockroach, partially dissected, to show electrodes in position at the ventral nerve cord and at the cercal nerve. A_5 and A_6 denote abdominal ganglia. Insets show impulses viewed on an oscilloscope.

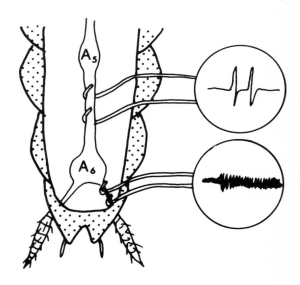

are not using the preamplifier, take the leads from the audio amplifier to the oscilloscope, as well as, to the speakers; this arrangement is not entirely satisfactory, but it works. These techniques will allow you to see nerve impulses on the oscilloscope screen.

Using only the audio amplifier, the sounds coming through the speaker are muted, as compared to the clear, loud sounds produced when a preamplifier stage is incorporated into the system. For best results, using only the audio amplifier, turn the treble level down and the base level up, and connect the input leads to the magnetic phono input jacks.

Prepare an anesthetized cockroach, pin it dorsal side up as in Exercise 4.2, dissect off the terga, and remove the digestive organs. Do not stretch or pin the ventral nerve cord! Immediately, fill the body cavity with mineral oil-saline solution (see Materials). Position the silver electrodes (about 8 mm apart) gently under the nerve cord (Fig. 5.14), lifting it slightly so that both electrodes are contacting the cord. Fix the electrode holder in place with modeling clay if it is not attached to a micromanipulator. Insert a third electrode into the thorax and connect it to the grounding jack on the amplifier. Connect the cables from the hooked electrodes to the input jacks on the amplifier. Remove the saline from the body cavity with a pipette to a level just below the hooked electrodes. Turn on the amplifier(s) and turn off all fluorescent lights that can practically be extinguished. Use an incandescent lamp if it is necessary to make alterations in the cockroach preparation.

Gently puff on the cerci using a soda straw. As nerve impulses travel up the nerve cord from wind receptors in the cerci the loudspeaker will deliver a loud 'hiss'. Touch the cerci with a wooden stick. What kind of stimuli are perceived by the cerci? Carefully remove the electrodes from the ventral nerve cord and replace them beneath and touching the cercal nerve (Fig. 5.14). Repeat the above procedure and notice that the sounds coming through the speaker are 'popping' noises rather than a loud 'hiss'. There are many more cercal nerves than there are giant axons in the nerve cord, and so the 'hiss' noise from the nerve cord represents a scaling down of the input from the cercal nerves through the last abdominal ganglion. If you record from the cercal nerve and then from the nerve cord, applying the same stimulus, you will note that the duration of impulses in the cercal nerve is longer than that in the nerve cord.

If a stimulator is available, place the stimulating electrode against the cercal nerve and apply an electrical pulse. Is the sound produced by the loudspeaker the same as the one evoked by blowing on the cerci? What does this suggest about the basis of nerve impulse propagation?

(2) Electroantennagram. A cockroach perceives odors through sensory cells on the antenna (Fig. 4.3). Nerve signals are transmitted to the brain in a code that is interpreted by the brain to determine what kind of odor and how much odor has been detected. As with the ventral nerve cord, we can 'listen' to signals transmitted from the sensory cells to the brain. An interesting odor to use in this experiment is female sex pheromone, which is known to stimulate sexual behavior in males. Directions for preparing sex pheromone are described in Exercise 6.5.

Excise the antenna of an adult male P. americana (females may be used as controls in sex pheromone tests). Place it in a wax dish under a dissecting microscope. Place one capillary electrode, with the chlorided-silver wire in place (see Methods), <u>over</u> the basal (cut) end of the antenna and seal this joint with paraffin. Cut the tip off of the antenna and place another capillary electrode over this end and seal the joint with paraffin. Fix the electrodes in place with modeling clay. At least 1.5 cm of antenna should still be exposed. Connect the electrodes to the input jacks of a DC preamplifier and connect the preamplifier to an audio amplifier with a speaker (and oscilloscope if one is to be used).

Connect plastic tubing from an air outlet to the cockroach preparation, terminating with a piece of glass tubing (approximately 0.5 cm diameter) pointed at the exposed portion of the antenna. The air should be filtered with glasswool and run through a water trap. Place a T-junction in the plastic tubing about 20-30 cm from the preparation and connect one end of a piece of plastic or glass tubing to the T and the other end to a 10 cc syringe. Odors are presented by placing a filter paper containing an odor solution (solvent evaporated) into a piece of glass tubing and inserting this 'cartridge' into the tubing adjacent to the syringe. When the syringe is depressed, a volume of air moves over the filter paper and into the air flow system. During the experiments an airflow of about 20-50 ml/sec is maintained in the plastic tubing, so that the antenna is constantly exposed to moving air. A simple alternative method is to deliver clean air to the antenna with a syringe, and then deliver odorous air with a syringe connected to an odor cartridge as described above.

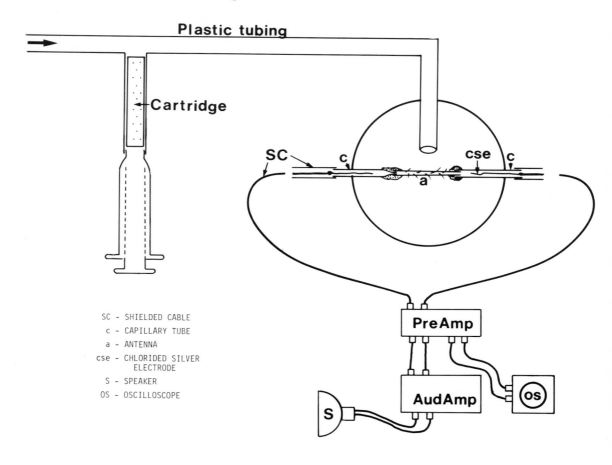

SC - SHIELDED CABLE
 c - CAPILLARY TUBE
 a - ANTENNA
cse - CHLORIDED SILVER
        ELECTRODE
 S - SPEAKER
OS - OSCILLOSCOPE

Turn on the amplifiers and listen to nerve impulses that are generated by antennal sensory cells when exposed to moving air and to odor molecules.

METHODS

Preparation of cerci and antennae. Cut off antennae and cerci from a newly molted white individual and place in a 0.5% solution of crystal violet (0.5 g in 100 ml distilled water). Soak until the hairs and spines are stained.

Hooked-electrodes. Shape silverwire into hook forms, solder to insulated wire. Insert each into a polyethylene sleeve (spaghetti) and then both into a larger sleeve to hold the two electrodes about 5 mm apart.

Chlorided sliver-capillary electrodes. (1) Rub a piece of 22-28 gauge silver wire with fine emery cloth. Place the end of the wire to be used as an electrode (the rubbed end) into a beaker of 0.2 M NaCl. Place another piece of silver wire (not to be an electrode) into the salt solution also. Connect the positive terminal of a 1.5 v battery to the electrode wire and the negative terminal to a 5 kohm resistor which is connected to the other silver wire. Allow the current to run about 30 minutes. Keep chlorided electrodes in a dark bottle filled with 0.2 M NaCl. (2) Pull a micropipette (capillary tubing) over a burner or on an electrode puller so that the tip is just large enough to accept the end of a cut antenna. Fill with cockroach saline. (3) Solder the non-chlorided end of the silver electrode to shielded cable and insert the electrode into the wide end of the capillary tube; the chlorided silver electrode must be bathed in the saline within the capillary. Bring the shielding of the cable slightly into the glass capillary and tape it firmly in place.

MATERIALS

Cockroaches (male and female Periplaneta)

Dissecting microscope, dissecting dish and instruments

Silver or tungsten 22-28 gauge wire electrodes (see Appendix II for sources)

Polyethylene tubing

Capillary tubing

Audio amplifier (50 - 100 Watts)

Speaker

DC preamplifier (antennae experiments) (Grass P16)

Preamplifier (ventral nerve cord) (Radio Shack 42-2930 or 42-2101; Lafayette 99-02198 or any ordinary Hi-fi preamp)

Stimulator (optional) (Grass SD9)

Oscilloscope (optional)

Shielded cable

Mineral oil (saline-mineral oil mixture: add 1 ml saline to 50 ml mineral oil; shake for 5 minutes; use immediately)

Incandescent lamp

Soda straws

Wooden application sticks

Aluminum foil

Wire and alligator clips

0.2 M NaCl

Emery cloth

Beaker

1.5 v battery

5 Kohm resistor

Female sex pheromone for Periplaneta americana (see Exercise 6.5), fruit odors, amylacetate

NOTES TO INSTRUCTOR

1. If you are picking up electrical noise that dwarfs the nerve impulses, construct a semisphere of aluminum foil to put over the preparation. Be sure to ground this shield with alligator slips connected to a water pipe. A Faraday cage, if available, will further decrease noise problems.
2. Oakley and Schafer (1978) and Miller (1979) provide further explanation of how to use electronic equipment in electrophysiological recording. Hoyle (1968) and Florey (1968) suggest additional experiments for cockroaches.

GENERAL READINGS

Florey, E. 1968. In: Experiments in Physiology and Biochemistry, Vol. 1, Ed. by G. A. Kerkut. New York: Academic Press.

Hansen, K. 1979. Insect chemoreception. In: Taxis and Behavior, Ed. by G. L. Hazelbauer. London: Chapman & Hall.

Hoyle, G. 1968. In: Experiments in Physiology and Biochemistry, Vol. 1, Ed. by G. A. Kerkut. New York: Academic Press.

Miller, T. A. 1979. Insect Neurophysiological Techniques. Heidelburg: Springer-Verlag.

Oakley, B. and Schafer, R. 1978. Experimental Neurobiology: A Laboratory Manual. Ann Arbor: Univ. Michigan Press.

Pearson, K. G. 1977. Interneurons in the ventral nerve cord of insects. In: Identified Neurons and Behavior of Arthropods, Ed. by G. Hoyle. New York: Plenum Press.

Pichon, Y. 1974. Axonal conduction in insects. In: Insect Neurobiology. Ed. by J. E. Treherne. New York: American Elsevier.

Pipa, R. L. and F. Delcomyn. 1981. Nervous system. In: The American Cockroach, Ed. by W. J. Bell and K. G. Adiyodi. London: Chapman & Hall.

Pringle, J. W. S. 1961. Proprioception in arthropods. In: The Cell and Organism. Ed. By J. H. Ramsey and V. B. Wigglesworth. Cambridge: University Press.

Seelinger, G. and T. Tobin. 1981. Sense Organs. In: The American Cockroach, Ed. by W. J. Bell and K. G. Adiyodi. London: Chapman & Hall.

Treherne, J. E. 1974. The environment and function of insect nerve cells. In: Insect Neurobiology, Ed. by J. E. Treherne. New York: American Elsevier.

RESEARCH REPORTS

Butler, R. 1973. The anatomy of the compound eye of Periplaneta americana L. I. General features. J. comp. Physiol. 83:223-238.

Chapman, K. M. 1965. Campaniform sensilla on the tactile spines of the legs of the cockroach. J. exp. Biol. 42:191-203.

Dagan, D. and I. Parnas. 1970. Giant fibre and small fibre pathways involved in the evasive response of the cockroach, Periplaneta americana. J. exp. Biol. 52:313-324.

Roeder, K. D. 1938. Organization of the ascending giant fiber system in the cockroach (Periplaneta americana). J. exp. Zool. 108:243-262.

Roth, L. M. and Barth, R. H. 1967. The sense organs employed by cockroaches in mating behavior. Behaviour 28:58-93.

Schafer, R. 1977. The nature and development of sex attractant specificity in cockroaches of the genus Periplaneta. IV. Electrophysiological study of attractant specificity and its determination by juvenile hormone. J. exp. Zool. 199:189-208.

Spencer, H. J. 1974. Analysis of the electrophysiological responses of the trochanteral hair receptors in the cockroach. J. exp. Biol. 60:233-240.

Toh, Y. 1977. Fine structure of antennal sense organs of the male cockroach, Periplaneta americana. J. Ultrast. Res. 60:373-394.

Washio, H. and C. Nishino. 1976. Electroantennogram responses to the sex pheromone and other odors in the American cockroach. J. Insect Physiol. 22:735-741.

Euphyllodromia *angustata* *(Blattellidae)* *in preparation*
for flight. Adults are 1.8 cm in length and feed on
hairs (trichomes) of leaves. Euphyllodromia is unusual
in that it is one of the few diurnal cockroaches. This
red, bronze and blue genus is commonly observed in the
tropics walking on vegetation and feeding during
daylight hours.

Exercise—5.9—LOCOMOTION: THE TRIPOD GAIT

How does an animal co-ordinate six legs for efficient locomotion? The answer can be found in our daily experience, because the 6-legged problem is not so different from the 4-legged (dog, cat, horse) problem. To discover the walking gait of a cockroach the experimenter must either keep the animal in one place, while allowing the legs to move in a normal manner, or record the footprints of an untethered animal.

A. <u>PREPARATION FOR OBSERVATIONS OF WALKING</u>. Fix a cockroach dorsally (using the largest, slowest species available) as described in Exercise 6.5. Attach the cockroach so that its legs are in contact with a piece of teflon or glass coated with silicone spray. The cockroach will walk or 'slide' on these substrata. A tripod gait with 3 legs engaged in a power stroke at one time will be observed (see Fig. 5.15).

Important rules for walking: (1) no leg is raised until the leg behind it is in a supporting position, and (2) the movements of the two legs of a segment must alternate. Each leg engages in a "power stroke" or <u>retraction</u> when it pushes against the substratum, and then a 'return stroke' or <u>protraction</u> when it is lifted and moved to another place.

To facilitate observations, position the cockroach upside-down and lower the glass plate against the legs. Using this method you can easily see the tarsi moving from one place to another.

B. <u>RECORDING LOCOMOTION</u>. Position a movie camera or video camera beneath or over the glass on which a cockroach walks to record movements of the legs. Analysis of the film will allow the experimenter to chart leg movements as shown in Fig. 5.15. To obtain data on the period of stepping, use a stop watch to record the time interval between power strokes of one leg. You will record the time, for example, when the right foreleg initiates a power stroke, and then record the time when this event occurs again.

C. <u>A SIMPLER METHOD FOR OBSERVING LOCOMOTION</u>. Another technique for recording the walking and running of cockroaches is to obtain a record of footprints. Smoked paper or paper coated with fine carbon dust will work to obtain footprints of a cockroach that runs over the paper. If you puff air on the cerci when the cockroach is half way across the paper, you can record both walking and running. The footprints can be examined most clearly if you place the paper on a piece of glass over a light.

D. <u>EXPERIMENTS WITH LOCOMOTION</u>. The following experiments stimulate cockroaches to execute changes in direction and walking speed. (1) Blow on the cerci to stimulate escape behavior (see also Exercise 6.5); (2) Remove or tie back (with thread) one or more legs to see if the gait is changed by the loss of participating legs in the tripod; (3) Position the set-up vertically or upside down; (4) Shine a light beam from one side to observe how a cockroach turns; (5) Ligature the 'neck' (as in Exercise 5.4) and cut off the head - can the cockroach still walk? Respond to air puffs? Is coordination of the legs affected? (6) Can cockroaches climb on any surface? How do they cling to a clean glass surface?

E. <u>JOINTS AND LEVERS</u>. Examine the way your bones move at the joints (articulation). For example, the first and second joints of each finger allow movement in only one direction (or plane); they are like 'hinges.' The joints at your shoulder and hip have a greater flexibility, owing to the ball and socket construction of the joint. Because all of the joints of the cockroach are external, and not internal as your own, they are very easy to observe. Try to describe the joints of cockroach legs and antennae by bending them in all potential directions. Are the joints of cockroaches analogous in structure and function to those in your body? If so, would you be willing to match your strength with that of a cockroach? You should be advised of the following information stated by Miall and Denny (1886): 'The force exerted by insects has long been remarked with surprise, and it is a fact familiar not only to naturalists, but to all observant persons, that making allowance for their small size, insects are the most powerful of common animals.'

The experiment must be devised so that you and the cockroach are tested in the same way. One way to carry out the test is to run a rope to a pulley and then down to a weight. You should be able to change the amount of weight hanging from the rope. You can tie the rope to your waist and determine how much weight you can lift. Start off by trying to lift a classmate who weighs about as much as you do. Now, for the cockroach, use the same mechanism, except a heavy thread will replace the rope. Start off using a wieght equal to that of the cockroach. Your data for yourself, and the cockroach (and other animals?) should be in terms of maximum weight lifted divided by the weight of the lifter. Which beast is stronger? Why?

MATERIALS

Adult cockroaches (large, slow walking preferred)
Glass plate (15 x 15 cm)
Silicon spray
Movie camera or video system (optional)
Soda straws
Ring stand

Stop watch
Pulley and rope
Fixed cockroach materials (see Exercise 6.5.)
Thread (for ligatures and wieght lifting)
Smoked paper (for kymograph) or fine carbon dust sprinkled on white paper

---

NOTES TO INSTRUCTOR

1. Using the footprint method students can record stepping patterns of beetles, worms, baby grasshoppers, ants or whatever animals are available.
2. This exercise can be combined with Exercise 6.5 on orientation (fixed cockroach preparation) if not all experiments in 6.5 are to be employed.
3. I have not included experiments on electrophysiological muscle recording because animals such as frogs and crayfish seem more appropriate than cockroaches for such experiments. Some experiments might be attempted with cockroaches, however, as suggested in several chapters of Kerkut (see Hoyle or Florey, Exercise 5.8, for reference), or other arthropods (Oakley and Schafer, 1978 - reference in Exercise 5.8); Miller (1979 - reference in Exercise 5.8) provides methods for recording from walking cockroaches.

GENERAL READINGS

Delcomyn, F. 1980. Neural basis of rhythmic behavior in animals. Science 210:292-498.

Fourtner, C. R. 1976. Central nervous control of cockroach walking. In: Neural Control of Locomotion, Ed. by R. M. Herman, S. Grillner, P. S.G. Stein, and D. G. Stuart. New York: Plenum Press.

Gray, J. 1957. How Animals Move. Edinburgh: R. & R. Clark Ltd. (Penguin Books).

Hughes, G. M. 1965. Locomotion: terrestrial. In: The Physiology of the Insecta, Ed. by M. Rockstein. New York: Academic Press.

Pearson, K. 1976. The Control of Walking. Sci. Amer. (Dec) pp. 72-77.

Wilson, D. M. 1966. Insect walking. Annu. Rev. Entomol. 11: 103-122.

RESEARCH REPORTS

Daley, D. L. and F. Delcomyn. 1980. Modulation of excitability of cockroach giant interneurons during walking. I. Simultaneous excitation and inhibition. J. Comp. Physiol. 138:231-239.

Delcomyn, F. and P. N. R. Usherwood. 1973. Motor activity during walking in the cockroach Periplaneta americana. I. Free Walking. J. exp. Biol. 59: 629-642.

Ewing, A. W. and A. Manning. 1966. Some aspects of the efferent control of walking in three cockroach species. J. Insect Physiol. 12: 1115-1118.

Hawkins, W. A. 1977. Effects of sex pheromone on locomotion in the male American cockroach, Periplaneta americana. J. Chem. Ecol. 4: 149-160.

Hughes, G. M. 1957. The coordination of insect movements. II. The effect of limb amputation and the cutting of commisures in the cockroach Blatta orientalis. J. exp. Biol. 34: 306-333.

Reingold, S. and Camhi, J. 1977. A quantitative analysis of rhythmic leg movements during three different behaviors in the cockroach Periplaneta americana. J. comp. Physiol. 23:1407-1420.

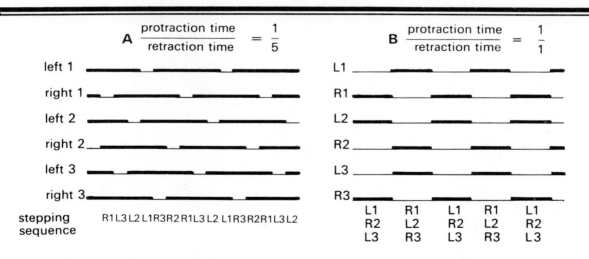

Fig. 5.15. Diagram showing the movements of the legs with different protraction/retraction time ratios. Thick lines: retraction, with the foot on the ground. Thin lines: protraction, with the foot in the air. Symbols: R = right, L = left; 1,2,3 = legs from anterior to posterior.

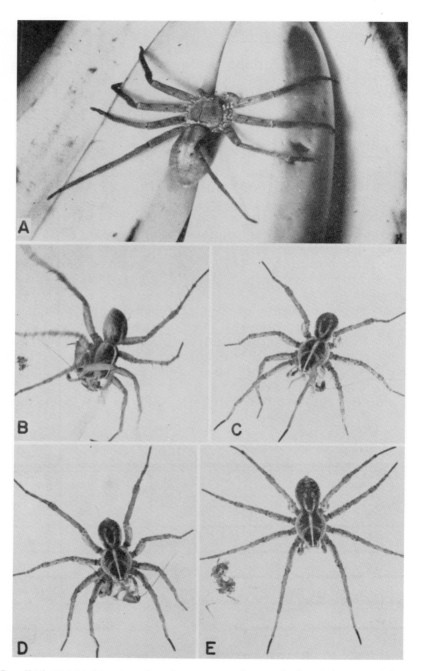

A, *Heteropoda venatoria*, a cockroach-hunting spider, slightly less than natural size, on bananas. B-E, *Lycosa* sp., a wolf spider, feeding on a nymph of *Supella longipalpa* in the laboratory.

Topic — **6** — BEHAVIORAL EXPERIMENTS

The cockroach is an excellent choice for many different kinds of behavioral experiments. One reason for its suitability is that it does not fly, hop or burrow; thus no special requirements are needed to reconstruct a relatively natural setting for an experiment. As with all animals, however, cockroaches become stressed when placed in experimental arenas or other devices. To compensate for this problem, keep in mind the necessity of allowing the cockroaches to become accustomed to your experimental setup before actually collecting data.

===

DATA BLANK I. Analysis of wall-seeking tendency

	Example from Fig. 6.1		Trial 1		Trial 2	
	#	o*	#	o*	#	o*
Total squares crossed						
Edge						
Non-edge						
	#	e*	#	e*	#	e*
Total squares in the arena						
Edge						
Non-edge						

$$\overline{X}^2 = \frac{(o - e)^2}{e} + \frac{(o - e)^2}{e} = .734^{**}$$

*Equals percent of edge or non-edge, e.g. 9/25, 16/25, 52/195, 143/195.

**The table in Appendix I shows that for this Chi-square value, there is no significant difference between observed and expected ratios; thus, there is no significant tendency for wall-seeking behavior in this example.

===

NOTES:

It is important to read the introduction to Appendix I and the section on Chi-square before using this statistical test to analyze your data.

Exercise—6.1—EXPLORATORY BEHAVIOR: RESPONSES TO NOVEL ENVIRONMENTS

Cockroaches exhibit certain types of behavior, as do many other animals, when placed in novel environments. These actions apparently are mechanisms to escape predation when cockroaches are moving in unfamiliar surroundings. One type of behavior, which is easily observed and recorded, is 'wall-seeking tendency.' The following procedure works equally as well with other walking insects, mice, newts or other small animals.

Experimental leads. Introduce a cockroach into the arena and record the grid squares traversed either by employing two observers, one to call out the code, the other to write down the sequence, or by using a tape recorder to record the sequence of grid squares traversed. To generate a 'printout' of the movements, the sequence of squares followed by the cockroach can be traced on a grid identical to that in the arena, but produced and duplicated on paper (Fig. 6.1). Does the cockroach stay close to the wall or are its movements random over the arena? Do cockroaches move in short bursts or do they maintain a steady gait? How often in a given time period do cockroaches enter the squares toward the center of the arena? What kinds of orientational movements are exhibited, e.g. looping? When the data are analyzed one could ask why cockroaches do what they do? Of what advantage are the types of behaviors observed? If you blow on the cockroach how does it respond, e.g. running to the edge or running to the center?

These experiments can be analyzed using simple statistical tests such as Chi-square (see also APPENDIX I): Insert the data obtained from arena experiments into the spaces provided in DATA BLANK I. The observed values (o) are from your observations. For example, in Fig. 6.1 the cockroach ran over 25 squares, 9 on the edge and 16 not on the edge; divide 9 and 16 by 25 to obtain the percent values for each (36% and 64%), and insert as shown. Now calculate the expected values (e). In Fig. 6.1 there are 195 total squares, 52 on the edge and 143 not on the edge; divide 52 and 143 by 195 to obtain the percent values (32% and 68%) and insert as shown. The next step is to use the Chi-square formula to determine if crossing 36% of the edge squares demonstrates a wall-seeking tendency, or if this performance could occur by chance.

METHODS

An arena for making observations on exploratory behavior can be square or round, but since cockroaches have a tendency to remain in corners, a round arena works best. Construct the floor of the arena with a piece of smooth wood painted with several coats of hard, white paint. Paint a grid onto the arena floor using a black magic marker to make 4 cm squares (Fig. 6.1). Code each square with a number and letter, such as A-1, C-33, etc. The arena is enclosed with a wall of metal or plastic garden trim, tacked to the edge of the plywood (see Materials section of Exercise 6.5).

MATERIALS

Arena
Stopwatch
Adult cockroaches; male <u>Blaberus</u>
  or <u>Leucophaea</u> preferred

Prepared grid patterns duplicated
  on paper
Tape recorder (optional)

GENERAL READINGS

Bell, W. J. 1981. Pheromones and behavior. In: <u>The American
    Cockroach</u>, Ed. by W. J. Bell and K. G. Adiyodi. London: Chapman &
    Hall.

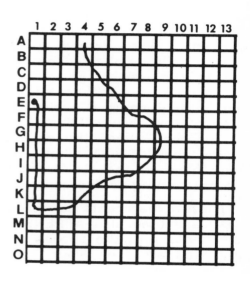

Fig. 6.1. Data sheet for recording movement of a cockroach through a gridded arena. The pathway shown is hypothetical, tracing an animal from E-1, along the wall to L-1, then into the center of the arena and back to A-4.

Exercise—6.2—LEARNING: SIMPLE TO COMPLEX TASKS

Cockroaches do not learn as quickly nor retain what they learned as long as some animals do. This apparent deficiency is partly related to the type of tasks normally encountered by cockroaches. Long-term learning could actually be counter-productive. A cockroach, for example, does not learn which large, vibration-making objects are potentially harmful and which are not; it runs quickly when it detects vibrations in the immediate environment.

A. <u>HABITUATION</u>. The simplest type of learning is the phenomenon whereby an animal stops responding to a stimulus that it initially responded to. Some animals, for example discriminate between nestmates and non-nestmates by becoming habituated to the odors of their nestmates. Strange conspecifics (members of the same species) are treated aggressively because the animals in a nest have not become habituated to the odors of the strangers. The nestmates have, in effect, 'learned' to discriminate nestmates from other individuals.

To investigate habituation, present cockroaches with the same stimulus at known intervals over an extended period of time. During this period, record the responses of the cockroaches to determine when they stop responding (DATA BLANK I). It is important to maintain the magnitude of the stimulus during testing, as an animal may habituate to one concentration of an odor or one intensity of vibration, but respond fully to another concentration or another intensity of vibration. Stimuli employed can be sounds (buzzer), vibrations (tapping on the cage), light (flashing), odors or other stimuli you might think of. Some of the odors employed in Exercises 6.3 and 6.4 would be entirely appropriate. Do cockroaches become habituated to all stimuli in about the same amount of time? Do you obtain different results if you increase the interval between stimulus applications? How could habituation to stimuli in the environment be advantageous or disadvantageous to cockroach survival?

B. <u>CORRECTING BEHAVIOR</u>. Another relatively simple type of learning involves the storage of information (in the nervous system) from proprioceptors in the appendages. Through such mechanisms animals 'record' a part of their locomotory history. For example, if a cockroach is moving in a certain direction and is forced to make a turn left or right, will the cockroach 'correct' for the previous turn and continue again in the original direction when the next chance for a turn is encountered? If so, how long can a cockroach 'remember' which turn must be taken to continue in the original direction?

An interesting series of experiments along these lines was published on millipedes. As a millipede walked through a plastic tube the investigator bent the tube (and the millipede within) to the left, and then straightened the tube. When the animal reached the opening it always 'corrected' by turning to the right. Moreover, the angle turned to the right was the same angle that the tube had been bent to the left.

A maze for studying cockroach correcting behavior can be constructed quite easily (see Fig. 6.2 and the Methods section). The first section of the maze, (A) in the figure, should provide a long corridor (about 25 to 50 cm) so that the cockroach will have a specific direction in which to move,

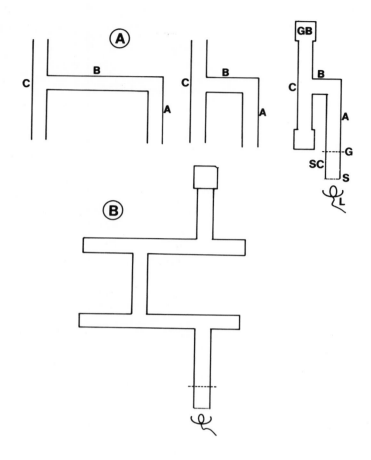

Fig. 6.2. (A) Maze for correcting behavior. Starting chamber, SC, is used to allow the cockroach to become accustomed to the tubing. A screen, S, prevents escape; a gate, G, of aluminum foil can be lifted to allow entry into the maze. An 8-watt bulb in a lamp, L, is turned on to urge the cockroach to move down corridor A. Corridor B can be exchanged for longer tubes as shown. At the ends of corridor C are 'goal boxes', GB, that can be removed when the cockroach enters.

(B) Complex maze for learning experiments (many other arrangements will work just as well).

and then a forced left or right choice, and then a corridor (B) that can be very short (2 cm) or long (20 cm) ending in a choice of a left or right turn into corridor (C). A cockroach which maintains its initial direction of movement through correcting behavior would be expected to turn left and then right. How long does the cockroach remember the direction of its previous turn? This can be determined by lengthening corridor (B). If the corridor is 20 cm long, will the cockroach still make the correct turn to maintain its initial direction? 200 cm long? Can cockroaches remember two or more turns? Errors can be plotted against length of corridor to quantify the results as shown in DATA BLANK II. Do not allow any individual to be tested successively with one maze pattern, as it will likely use this experience to avoid making incorrect turns.

C. LEARNING NOT TO CORRECT. If you use the maze in section B, but put the cockroach shelter at the left end of corridor (C) will the cockroach, after several successive trials learn by association to turn left instead of correcting to the right? The shelter or food and water at the left end of corridor (C) represent positive reinforcements, whereas you could provide negative reinforcement, such as a bright light or an electric shock (12 volt battery grid) at the right end of corridor (C). Errors can be recorded at the turn, and, as one might expect, the errors diminish over time. Once the maze is learned, how long does the cockroach remember? This question can be answered by training individual cockroaches until the maze is learned, and then wait a few hours, a day, or longer before running the individual again. Plot these results in DATA BLANK III. (The maze should be washed between each trial to eliminate odor clues.)

D. LEARNING WITHOUT A BRAIN. A rather difficult, but rewarding project-type experiment, is to test the learning capabilities of one cockroach leg and its thoracic ganglion. Basically the leg is severed from the body, but with the nerve and the thoracic ganglion kept intact. The nerves are maintained in cockroach saline, and the leg is clamped by the femur to a ring stand. A beaker of saline, equipped with an open electrical circuit, is positioned so that the leg dips into the saline when the leg relaxes. The leg will relax, the experimenter gives it an electrical shock, and the leg learns to maintain a position just above the surface of the liquid. Questions arise as to whether learning is accelerated or longer-lasting when the whole animal (including the head) is intact. Why do cockroaches have heads? Since this experiment requires a more detailed description, the reader should consult the references listed on this subject.

METHODS

A maze for the purpose described here will work best if constructed from tubular material. In a maze corridor with a square cross-section the cockroach may walk on the sides or on top, thus biasing turns at junctions. Tubes, however, are difficult to connect at T-junctions. One method is to use plastic hamster runways that are sold in pet stores. A better method is to purchase plastic PVC joints (elbows, Ts, etc, as used in do-it-yourself plumbing), glass tubing (from a supplier or a glass blower), plastic or plexiglas tubing (from plastic companies), or roll your own tubes using plastic sheeting (storm window material) and transparent tape. Fit the tubes into the PVC joints to construct a temporary maze pattern.

==

DATA BLANK I. Habituation curve

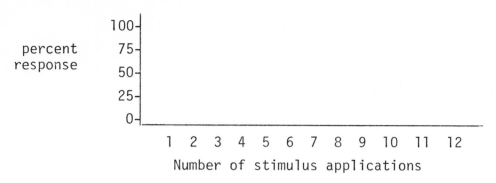

==

DATA BLANK II. Correcting behavior curve

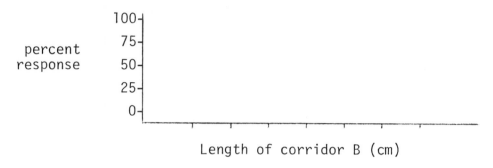

==

DATA BLANK III. Learning by association curve

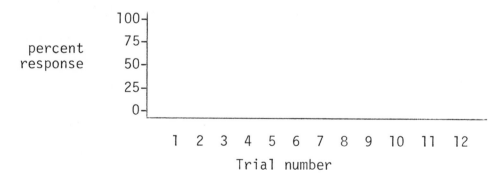

==

NOTES:

*(1) Compare habituation curves for various kinds of stimuli
      (light, sound vibrations, odors) or different stimulus intensities
      (turning on a 10-, 25-, 50- or 100-watt bulb).*

*(2) Compare correcting ability among nymphs, males and females.
      The Mann-Whitney U-test can be used to compare percent responses
      for a designated corridor length (see Appendix I).*

MATERIALS

Cockroaches (any species, nymphs are best for mazes; milkweed bugs or beetles can be substituted)
Odorants (pheromones, amyl acetate, irritants)
Devices for producing sounds, vibrations, etc.
Maze materials
8-Watt lamp
Stop watch
12-volt battery and grid (optional)

Optional leg-learning materials: cockroach saline, dissecting instruments, ring stand, beakers, wire, clips; see references for more details.

NOTES TO INSTRUCTOR

1. Clever students will quickly discover that individual cockroaches have turning tendencies (left or right). Thus maze experiments are not usually as simple as the novice investigator initially suspects. Good controls for each animal may be required.
2. In habituation experiments, students should first determine the nature of responses to various stimuli that might be applied.

GENERAL READINGS

Alloway, T. M. 1972. Learning and memory in insects. Annu. Rev. Entomol. 17: 43-56.
McConnell, J. V. 1966. Comparative physiology: learning in invertebrates. Annu. Rev. Physiol. 28: 107-136.

RESEARCH REPORTS

Akre, R. D. 1964. "Correcting" behavior by insects on vertical and horizontal mazes. J. Kans. Entomol. Soc. 37: 169-186.
Dingle, H. 1962. The occurrence of correcting behavior in various insects. Ecology 43: 727-728.
Eisenstein, E. M. 1972. Learning and memory in isolated insect ganglia. Adv. Insect Physiol. 9: 111-181.
Eisenstein, E. M. and M. J. Cohen. 1965. Learning in an isolated prothoracic in insect ganglion. Anim. Behav. 13: 104-108.
Horridge, G. A. 1962. Learning of leg position by the ventral nerve cord in headless insects. Proc. R. Soc. Lond. (B) 157: 33-52.
Horridge, G. A. 1975. The electrophysiological approach to learning in an isolatable ganglia. Anim. Behav. (Suppl) 1: 163-182.
Longo, N. 1970. A runway for the cockroach (Periplaneta sp.) Behav. Res. Methods Instrument. 2: 118-119.
Lovell, K. L. and E. M. Eisenstein. 1973. Dark avoidance learning and memory disruption by carbon dioxide in cockroaches. Physiol. & Behav. 10: 835-840.
Willner, P. 1978. What does the headless cockroach remember? Anim. Learn. Behav. 6: 249-257.

Archroblatta (Blaberidae) *sp. is an ochre and yellow Blaberid that is usually found in the rain forest canopy. Here it is shown feeding on algae and fungi that grow on leaves.*

Exercise– 6.3 –AGGREGATION AND SOCIAL INTERACTIONS

Individuals of a given species may come together for a variety of reasons, but usually aggregation affords some type of protection. Examples of aggregation are schooling in fish, flocking in birds, cummunes of certain kinds of bees, and grouping in secluded locations by cockroaches. One might ask, what mechanism operates to assist individuals in forming an aggregate? We know that visual and vibrational cues are important to fish swimming in schools; what cues are available to cockroaches for aggregation? Studies have shown that most species of domiciliary cockroaches secrete an aggregation pheromone in their feces; this is an odor which is used by cockroaches to recognize appropriate sites of aggregation. Aggregation implies, however, that cockroaches are <u>attracted</u> to the pheromone source, and in the presence of the pheromone, their <u>locomotion is inhibited</u>. The following experiments test these assumptions.

A. <u>AGGREGATION BEHAVIOR</u>. First, some initial observations should be made with adults and nymphs to better understand the phenomenon of aggregation. This can be accomplished by placing the insects in cages or aquaria with no shelters and watching for a short time. When the shelters previously used by the cockroaches are replaced, the insects will quickly move inside. If new (clean) shelters are used instead, the cockroaches will not be immediately attracted to them, and will explore the new shelters before entering. These observations suggest that sensory cues are present in the shelters that cockroaches have previously used.

B. <u>AGGREGATION PHEROMONE</u>. To answer the question 'are cockroaches attracted to their shelters because of an aggregation pheromone?' it is necessary to perform a chemical extraction. Add 1 gram of 'chopped up shelter' or feces to 1 ml of methanol, allowing it to soak in a covered vessel for 24 hours; filter out sediment and shelter material; keep in the refrigerator if possible. The next task is to design a bioassay to test the attractive qualities of the extract on cockroaches. The following bioassay procedure, developed by Ishii and Kuwahara (1967), is one of several methods that can be used.

Cut filter paper into 3 x 7 cm strips and fold to make 'W's as shown in Fig. 6.3. The strips are dipped in either the extract (experimental) or methanol (control). Allow both kinds of strips to set out, where there are no cockroaches, for 3 hours. Place 3 folded strips (one experimental and two controls) in a dish, add about 20 first instar nymphs and cover. A white piece of paper under the dish will make viewing easier. After 15 minutes count the number of cockroaches on each strip and insert the results in DATA BLANK I. The expected number of insects on the experimental strip is 33% of the total, and so a Chi-square statistical test can be used to determine if the cockroaches were attracted or repelled to any substances on the strips (refer to Appendix I for details on Chi-square tests). The time required for aggregation can be quantitatively determined by taking readings at every min and plotting the number of cockroaches on the extract-impregnated strip over time (DATA BLANK II). The distance of attraction can be measured by employing dishes of different sizes (DATA BLANK III).

C. <u>IS VISION INVOLVED IN AGGREGATION</u>. In the initial experiment with shelters, both visual cues and olfactory cues were present in terms of

==

DATA BLANK I. Aggregation preferences

Trial #	1	2	3	4	5	Total	% of total	% expected
Control 1								
Control 2								
Pheromone								

Total:

==

DATA BLANK II. Time required for aggregation

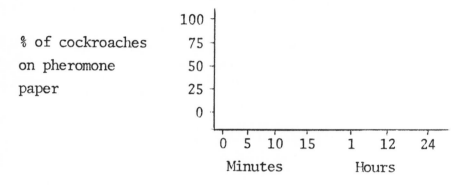

% of cockroaches
on pheromone
paper

==

DATA BLANK III. Effect of dish size (attraction index)

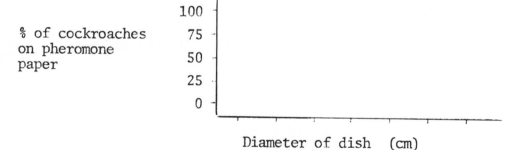

% of cockroaches
on pheromone
paper

==

NOTES:

There are other ways to express the data collected in these experiments. Keep in mind that the extent of aggregation will differ over _time_*, and that you will also find differences according to the* _variables_ *that you test (e.g. different sizes of arenas).*

dark spots created by defecation and odors from the feces. The role of vision can be tested by putting brown and yellowish spots (with water color paint) on filter paper strips used in the assay. For example, you could test the following triad of papers: (1) aggregation pheromone only, (2) aggregation pheromone with spots and (3) spots only. Is there an additive effect of visual and olfactory cues on aggregation?

D. INTERACTION AMONG INDIVIDUALS AS A FACTOR IN AGGREGATION

Set up aggregation tests using three control papers (or) three pheromone treated papers. Do the cockroaches sort out approximately equally on all three papers? Generate a frequency distribution chart for the number of cockroaches on all papers in 10 tests. How do you explain the unequal distributions? By watching individual cockroaches locating the filter papers and each other, you may form testable hypotheses relating to the role of social interactions in aggregation.

E. OTHER VARIABLES.

Do all cockroach species have the same aggregation pheromone? Test nymphs of species A with aggregation pheromone of species B. Do cockroaches aggregate to a greater extent during the day than at night? Why are 'W-shaped' filter papers used in the assay? Would other shapes work as well?

MATERIALS

Blattella or Periplaneta nymphs
 (first instars are best) and adults
Nymphs of other cockroach species
 (optional)
Filter paper (Whatman #1)

Scissors
Finger bowls (or 100 ml equivalent)
Methanol
Water color paints

NOTES TO INSTRUCTOR

1. First instar nymphs (those that hatch from the ootheca) should be used in aggregation assays.
2. If extraction is not possible, simply place 'W'-shaped filter papers in cockroach colonies for several days to impregnate them with aggregation pheromone.

GENERAL READINGS

Bell, W. J. 1981. Pheromones and behavior. In: The American Cockroach, Ed. by W. J. Bell and K. G. Adiyodi. London: Chapman & Hall.
Persoons, C. J. and F. J. Ritter. 1979. Pheromones of cockroaches. In: Chemical Ecology, Odour communication in Animals, Ed. by F. J. Ritter. Amsterdam: Elsevier/North Holland Biomedical Press.

RESEARCH REPORTS

Bell, W. J., Parsons, C., and E. A. Martinko. 1972. Cockroach aggregation pheromones: analysis of aggregation tendency and species specificity. J. Kans. Entomol. Soc. 45: 414-420.

Burk, T. and W. J. Bell. 1973. Cockroach aggregation pheromone: inhibition of locomotion (Orthoptera: Blattidae). J. Kans. Entomol. Soc. 46: 36-41.

Ishii, S. 1970. An aggregation pheromone of the German cockroach Blattella germanica (L): II. Species specificity of the pheromone. Appl. Entomol. Zool. 5:33-41.

Ishii, S. and Kuwahara, Y. 1967. An aggregation pheromone of the German cockroach Blattella germanica (L) (Orth. Blattellidae). I. Site of the pheromone production. Appl. Entomol. Zool. 2:203-217.

Ishii, S. and Kuwahara, Y. 1968. Aggregation of German cockroach Blattella germanica nymphs. Experienta 24:88-89.

Izutsu, M., Ueda, S. O. and Ishii, S. 1970. Aggregation effects on the growth of the German cockroach, Blattella germanica (L.) (Blattaria, Blattellidae). Appl. Entomol. Zool. 5:159-171.

Roth, L. M. and Cohen, S. 1973. Aggregation in Blattaria. Annals. Entomol. Soc. Amer. 66: 1315-1323.

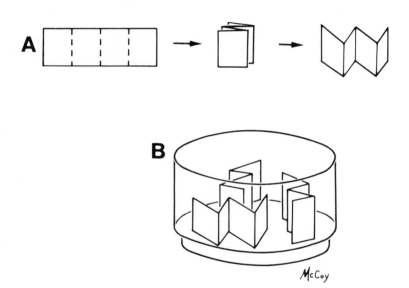

Fig. 6.3. Instructions for preparing the aggregation assay 'arena': (A) Fold 3 × 7 cm filter paper strips into 'W' forms, (B) place strips upright into a finger bowl and cover.

Exercise— 6.4 —SEX PHEROMONES AND SEXUAL BEHAVIOR

Species-specific odors are used by a variety of insect species (and other animals such as deer, wolves, and rats) to convey information from one individual to another. Typical information cues include alarm, territorial marking, sexual receptivity, sex (I am male or female) and age. Orientation and sexual behavior stimulated by sex pheromones are spectacular types of behavior that are well illustrated by cockroaches. The objective of the following series of experiments is to investigate and to quantify the components of sexual behavior in <u>Periplaneta</u> <u>americana</u>.

A. <u>FEMALE SEX PHEROMONE</u>. The first step is to obtain a source of sex pheromone by placing a filter paper disk (~ 5.5 cm diameter) in a container holding one or more virgin female cockroaches. Select and isolate last instar nymphs (the largest non-adult individuals in the colonies--see Box #1). Each day remove the newly emerged females and place them in mason jars with filter paper disks. Within 10 days they begin to secrete sex pheromone and will continue for at least two weeks if they remain virgin. For testing sex pheromone, isolate a group of males in a cage away from females and sex pheromone. To assay for sex pheromone the following technique can be utilized.

B. <u>SEX PHEROMONE BIOASSAY</u>. Place five isolated male cockroaches in a cage or shoe box approximately 16 x 25 cm. The more cages used in an assay the more reliable the results will be. Draw a line across the bottom of the cage as shown in Fig. 6.4 (see Exercise 6.7).   The behavior used in this assay is increased rate of locomotion of males stimulated by sex pheromone. The idea is to count the number of times each of five male cockroaches crosses the line during each minute following the introduction of sex pheromone. Control values, obtained with solvent only, are subtracted from experimental values. Fig. 6.5 is a plot of line crosses or activity counts per min (ACPM) calculated from assays with a serial dilution of the synthetic female sex pheromone of <u>Periplaneta</u> <u>americana</u>, periplanone B.

C. <u>SEX PHEROMONE EXTRACTION</u>. Place strips of filter paper (3 x 12 cm) in the cage containing virgin females. After one week, remove the papers, roll them together into a tight coil and soak in a volume of n-hexane that covers the papers (Fig. 6.6). Cork the tube. After 2 hours remove the hexane and refill. Add both aliquots to a test tube. Now, test for sex pheromone by putting 0.5 ml of the solution onto a 5.5 cm filter paper disk and using the disk in the bioassay (Section B). If the activity obtained is greater than 20 ACPM you can use the solution without further labor. If the activity recorded is very low, concentrate the solution in one of the following ways. If a vacuum apparatus is available, reduce the solution to about 0.5 ml. If a vacuum apparatus is not available, place the solution in warm water (30° C) in a hood and allow it to evaporate to about 1.0 ml; swirl the solution during evaporation. If nitrogen gas is available, run nitrogen through a pasteur pipette into the tube at a rate so that the hexane surface vibrates slightly during evaporation. Keep the stock sex pheromone in a refrigerator. For testing, 0.1 ml will probably suffice; even better, test aliquots of a serial dilution to find the minimum quantity that will stimulate male cockroaches.

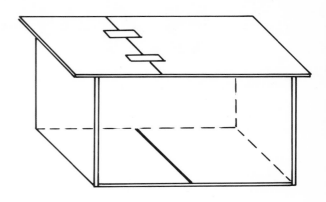

Fig. 6.4. Plastic mouse cage with hinged top for assaying female sex pheromone. Line is drawn on the bottom of the cage to measure activity of males stimulated by pheromone.

Fig. 6.5. Line crossing represented as activity counts per minute (ACPM) of males responding to different concentrations (in micrograms) of synthetic female sex pheromone, periplanone B, over a test period of 5 min. P signifies 'pre-exposure' activity. Each point represents the average of 10 tests with cages of 5 cockroaches. Vertical lines are standard deviations.

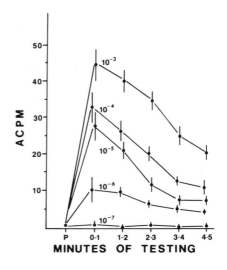

Fig. 6.6. Filter papers in a test tube with hexane.

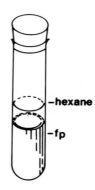

D. SEX PHEROMONE-STIMULATED ORIENTATION AND COURTSHIP BEHAVIOR. When virgin females, isolated males and sex pheromone are all available, the following experiments can be attempted.

(1) Chemo-orientation. Place a sex pheromone-impregnated filter paper in the center of an arena (see Exercise 6.5). Release a male at the periphery, observe its orientation to the pheromone source, and record the time required for the male to find the source. To reduce the role of vision, illuminate the arena with low intensity blacklight (50 Watts) and put a dot of blacklight-reflecting paint on the back of each cockroach, (or) use absolute darkness and dots of phosphorescent paint on the cockroaches, (or) use dim white light and paint the floor of the arena the same color as the pheromone-impregnated filter paper disk. Some variables: remove one or both antennae to determine if the antennae are required for locating an odor source; try different pheromone concentrations or different aged males. Further experimental ideas on the topic of orientation are described in Exercise 6.5.

(2) Courtship behavior. Courtship behavior can be stimulated in either of two ways. First, if males are provided only with sex pheromone, one can observe the behavior that is elicited exclusively by olfactory stimuli. Second, by pairing males and virgin females one can observe the sequences of male and female courtship acts and copulation. Of interest is the variation in sequences, the role of contact pheromones and specific tactile signals that are important releasers of behavior. A basic scheme for courtship behavior in Periplaneta is depicted in Fig. 6.7.

E. EFFECT OF MATING ON PHEROMONE PRODUCTION. Females presumably produce and secrete sex pheromone to attract and excite males. Do they waste resources by producing pheromone after they have mated? Place the females that have been mated in Section D.2 in isolation (mason jars, if available) with a filter paper disk. Test the filter paper in the male assay (Section B) every other day and put the females into clean jars (pheromone sticks to glass). Does pheromone production decrease?

MATERIALS

Colony of virgin, newly molted
    female Periplaneta americana
Plastic cages (16 x 25 x 16) or shoe
    boxes (Disposable mouse cages are
    available from laboratory suppliers)
Stop watch
Magic marker (black)
Hand counter (optional)
Filter paper disks, (5.5 cm
    diameter, Whatman #1)
Pasteur pipettes and bulb
n-hexane (pentane can be substituted)

Acetone
Test tubes (5 ml or smaller)
Mason jars
Forceps
Black light bulb and blacklight-
    reflecting paint
Arena (see Exercise 6.5)
Optional materials for extraction:
    50 µl pipettes (optional)
    Compressed nitrogen tank (optional)
    Vacuum pump or source of vacuum
        (optional)
    Vacuum jar (optional)

1. All experiments can be performed using only the filter papers removed from a cage of virgin females. Use of extracted sex pheromone simply eliminates all non-chemical cues and adds a quantitative approach that is not possible with filter papers.

2. It is important to wash forceps and other instruments in two rinses of acetone after contact with females or filter papers impregnated with sex pheromone.

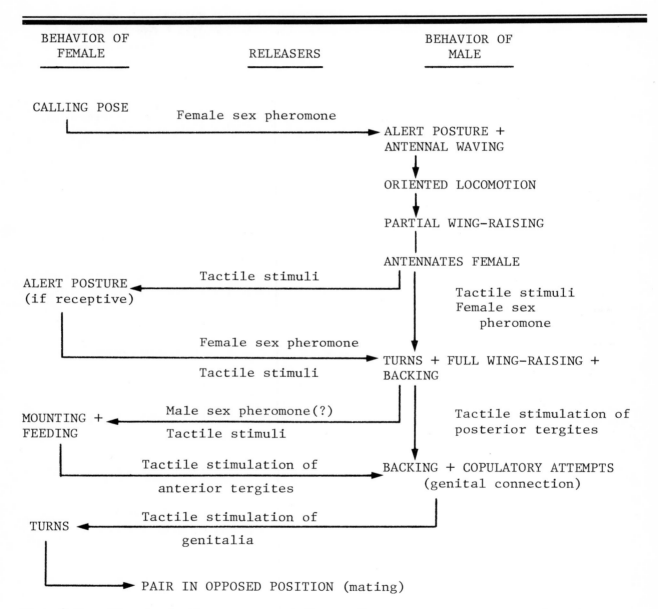

Fig. 6.7. Diagrammatic representation of common sequences in the courtship of Periplaneta americana. Releasers are sensory cues that stimulate specific behavioral actions; the term 'tactile' indicates a mechanical stimulus, such as antennation.

GENERAL READINGS

Bell, W. J. 1981. Pheromones and Behavior. In: The American Cockroach, Ed. by W. J. Bell and K. G. Adiyodi. London: Chapman & Hall.

Roth, L. M. and E. R. Willis. 1952. A study of cockroach behavior. Amer. Midl. Nat. 47: 66-129.

Shorey, H. H. 1976. Animal Communication by pheromones. New York: Academic Press.

Wilson, E. O. 1963. Pheromones. Sci. Amer. (May) pp. 163-172.

RESEARCH REPORTS

Barth, R. H. Jr. 1964. The mating behavior of Byrsotria fumigata (Guérin) (Blattidae, Blaberinae). Behaviour 23: 1-30.

Barth, R. H. 1970. The mating behavior of Periplaneta americana (Linnaeus) and Blatta orientalis Linnaeus (Blattaria, Blattinae), with notes on 3 additional species of Periplaneta and interspecification of female sex pheromones. Z. Tierpsychol. 27: 722-748.

Bell, W. J., Burns, R. E. and R. H. Barth. 1974. Quantitative aspects of the male courting response in the cockroach Byrsotria fumigata (Guérin) (Blattaria). Behav. Biol. 10: 419-433.

Hawkins, W. A. 1978. Effects of sex pheromone on locomoation in the male American cockroach Periplaneta americana. J. Chem. Ecol. 4: 149-160.

Hawkins, W. A. and M. K. Rust. 1977. Factors influencing male sexual response in the American cockroach Periplaneta americana. J. Chem. Ecol. 3: 85-99.

Rust, M. K. 1976. Quantitative analysis of male responses released by female sex pheromone in Periplaneta americana. Anim. Behav. 24: 681-684.

Rust, M. K., Burk, T. and W. J. Bell. 1976. Pheromone-stimulated locomotory and orientation responses in the American cockroach. Anim. Behav. 24: 52-67.

Wharton, D. R. A., Miller, G. L. and M. L. Wharton. 1954a. The odorous attractant of the American cockroach, Periplaneta americana (L.). I. Quantitative aspects of the response to the attractant. J. gen. Physiol. 37: 461-469.

Wharton, D. R. A., Miller, G. L. and M. L. Wharton. 1954b. The odorous attractant of the American cockroach, Periplaneta americana (L.). II. A bioassay method for the attractant. J. gen. Physiol. 37: 471-481.

Exercise–**6.5**—SPATIAL ORIENTATION: DIRECTED MOVEMENTS

Animals move in their environment in order to locate resources and to avoid stress. They also move their bodies to maintain a normal position. All of these activities are included in the term spatial orientation. Some of the chapters in this book have already included some aspects of orientation (sexual behavior, aggregation exploration, maintenance), and many stimuli that can be tested in orientation experiments (pheromones, light) have already been discussed. This section deals in part with methodology that will assist the investigator in designing orientation experiments. The objective is to observe directional movements of cockroaches with respect to stimuli that are presented in the environment. There are basically two ways to carry out these kinds of experiments: allowing the cockroach to orient in an arena or other type of containment and fixing the cockroach so that it turns or 'walks on' a styrofoam ball. Both techniques have problems: the arena is restrictive and requires some way to record orientation pathways; the fixed preparation is somewhat unnatural and therefore subject to experimental artefacts. Good planning, however, can overcome some of these problems.

A. ESCAPE BEHAVIOR. Most predators generate wind currents when they lunge (rat) or flick their tongue (toad) at a cockroach (Fig. 6.8). If you simulate these tell-tale wind puffs with a pipette bulb, syringe or soda straw, you can see how quickly the cockroach responds. What are the organs that perceive wind puffs?

To investigate escape behavior, either an arena or a fixed preparation can be employed (see Methods). By directing puffs at 360° around the animal, and observing responses, it should be possible to determine approximately where the sensory organs are located. One or both suspected sensory organs can be removed or coated with wax. Depending on the equipment available, investigators can determine how the cockroach determines the direction of the attack.

B. VERTICAL ORIENTATION. During the active and inactive phases of the photocycle, do cockroaches prefer to move upwards or downwards on a vertical wall? What direction do they follow if a wind puff is directed at them? Place a cardboard box, with one side removed, into a cage of cockroaches to allow observations of cockroaches on vertical and horizonal surfaces. By checking the cockroaches over time it should be possible to generate a graph relating the relative preferences of vertical and horizontal surfaces (DATA BLANK I). Are preferences of males and females the same? How do these preferences correlate with adaptations for survival?

C. ATTRACTION AND REPULSION. Female sex pheromone was shown in Exercise 6.5 to attract male Periplaneta. Using the styrofoam Y-maze, the male cockroach can be easily manipulated for experiments with sex pheromone positioned in front of or to the side of a cockroach. In the arena, with an odor source on filter paper in the center, the orientation pathways of male cockroaches can be filmed and studied in detail. Test various odorants off the shelf to discover possible cockroach repellants.

D. ORIENTATION IN DARK/LIGHT. To give cockroaches a choice-situation, construct borders for the arena or fixed-cockroach preparation with black and white cardboard or use a light on one side and

115

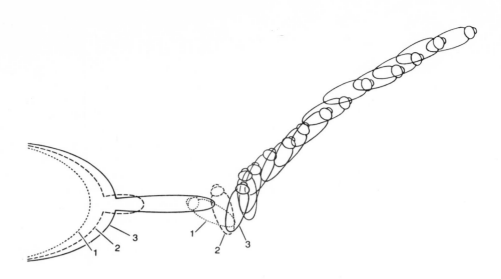

Fig. 6.8. Motion picture sequence of the tongue of a toad (left) and the escaping cockroach (right). The numbers represent frames of motion picture film, 1 being the first frame in the sequence, and 3 showing that the cockroach has moved away and out of reach of the toad's fully extended tongue. Frames are shown at 16-millisecond intervals.

Fig. 6.9. Apparatus for testing thigmotaxis. Constructed from a piece of dowel and circles of cardboard. The spacings increase and decrease from the top down to insure that height is not a factor in spacing choices.

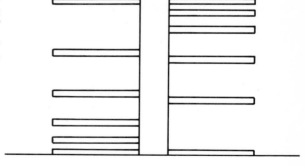

no light on the other. Determine the preferences of cockroaches and analyze the data statistically (Appendix I).

A simpler method for choice-tests is to use Petri dishes. For example, paint one half of the cover black. Put 5 small nymphs in the dish and turn on an overhead light. After 5 min count the number of cockroaches in each half of the dish and compare with the data gathered from control tests (with unpainted or completely painted covers). Data can be inserted into DATA BLANK II.

E. PATTERNS. What types of visual patterns are cockroaches attracted to? One simple dichotomy is to employ vertical and horizontal stripes. Perhaps horizontal stripes will be preferred, since they are similar to edges which cockroaches run toward when frightened. What about circles vs squares? Can you design patterns that you predict would be more attractive to cockroaches than other patterns?

F. THIGMOTAXIS. Some animals prefer to rest with their bodies touching other objects, a preference that is called thigmotaxis. To test this behavior with cockroaches, build a 'compartment house' in which each compartment has a different height between the floor and ceiling (Fig. 6.9). The 'living space' should vary from 1 to 4 cm in height (or according to the sizes of cockroaches tested). Count the number of cockroaches residing in each compartment each day, and place the data in DATA BLANK III. For each test, be sure to use a group of adults or a group of nymphs, because the size of the individuals will determine their preference. How quickly do cockroaches locate their preferred compartments?

METHODS

Arena construction. The easiest way to build an arena is to go to the local metal worker shop (air conditioning, heating) and order a piece of thin gauge metal (whatever is cheapest) about 24 cm wide and a length equal to the circumference of a circle you wish to enclose. Bolt or rivet the two ends together, lay it down on a piece of white or brown wrapping paper or directly on the floor, and you have an arena. Add a thin layer of petroleum jelly to prevent escapes. For a more portable unit, nail the lower sides of the arena to a circular piece of 3/4 inch plywood or composition board.

Procedures for arena studies. Responses of cockroaches to odors such as sex pheromone, repellants, insecticides, food or water can be tested by placing sources of these stimuli in the center of the arena and recording pathways taken by the cockroach.

To prevent cockroaches from using vision in the arena (if that is necessary for your experiment), use one of the following techniques: (1) Illuminate the arena with blacklight (disco lighting) and put a 1 cm dot of blacklight paint on the pronotum of the cockroach; (2) Illuminate the arena with dim white light, placing a 1 m high fence around the arena to block out objects outside the arena, and paint the arena floor the same color as the odor-containing filter paper (white?) used in the experiment; (3) Run experiments in total darkness and put a dot of phosphorescent (glow in the dark) paint on the cockroach.

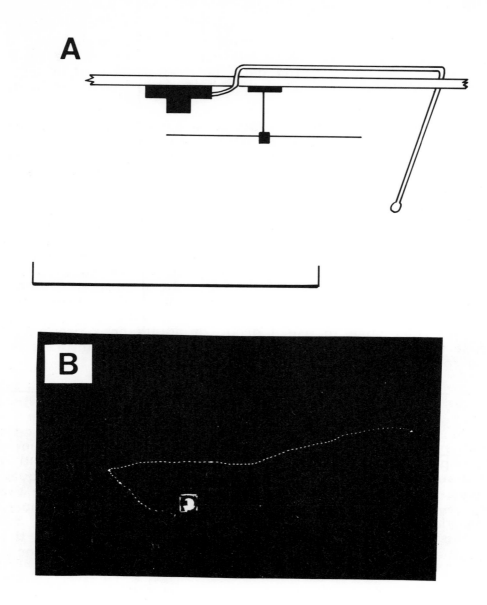

Fig. 6.10. (A) Diagram of an arena, camera and chopper for recording orientation pathways. (B) Example of 'dots' produced on film of a cockroach walking in an arena; larger 'dots' represent pauses.

To record the pathways one needs to use either a camera or a system of mirrors to focus the arena on a large piece of paper. The camera technique is actually simpler to set up than a mirror system. One needs only to mount a single-lens-reflex, 35 mm, camera above the arena (wide angle lens recommended for large arenas) and hook up a trigger-device to activate the shutter (Fig. 6.10A). An air bulb and air tube system is an inexpensive shutter release; electronic triggers and motor-drive units are more expensive, but allow many frames to be successively exposed. Time-lapse photos of 20 sec to 1 min exposure are taken, using Tri-x black and white ASA 400 film. The cockroach shows up on the film as a streaky line. If a 'chopper,' turned by a motor, is positioned beneath the camera lens, the resulting pathway will be a series of dots (Fig. 6.10B). The 'chopper' is a slotted disk that periodically blocks the camer lens when the solid part of the disk is beneath it.

Alternatives to the SLR: (1) A movie camera can be employed instead of the SLR camera if suitable lenses are available. (2) A video camera system will record cockroach orientation patterns even under dim red or white light, and students can watch the behavior on a monitor. (3) If equipment for photographing orientation pathways is not available, use the tracking methods described in Exercise 5.9. Fine carbon dust on white paper or smoked paper will reveal 'footprints' in an arena experiment.

Fixed -cockroach methods. Fix a cockroach dorsally (after removing its wings) to a 7 cm piece of 3 mm dowel or to a piece of cardboard (Fig. 6.11). Attachments will adhere to the cockroach cuticle with Scotch Spraymount; spray the adhesive onto a piece of aluminum foil, then use a matchstick to gather up a drop for fixing the cockroach. Once the adhesive is dry, the cockroach can be picked up and clamped to a beaker holder, clothes pin, hemostat or other device. A styrofoam ball (used for Christmas decorations) is brought up under the cockroach and grasped by its legs. After a few moments the cockroach makes walking movements, turning the ball, and quickly becomes accustomed to this mode of walking. It will even 'walk' in this manner upside down. The trick in using a styrofoam ball is to reduce its weight by cutting it in half with a razor saw, hollowing out the styrofoam with sandpaper into a sphere with 2 mm walls, and gluing it back together with white glue!

Fig. 6.11. Tethered cockroach 'walking' on a sytrofoam y-maze globe. The tethering stick that is glued to the cockroach would, in actuality, by attached to a clamp for support.

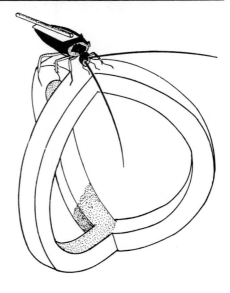

119

===

DATA BLANK I. Preferences for vertical <u>vs</u> horizontal surfaces

Day of testing:		1	2	3	4	5	6	%	expected %
Number of animals on:	horizontal								50
	vertical								50

===

DATA BLANK II. Preferences for light <u>vs</u> dark chambers of Petri dishes

Test number:		1	2	3	4	5	6	%	expected %
Number of animals in:	Dark								50
	Light								50

===

DATA BLANK III. Thigmotactic preferences of adult cockroaches

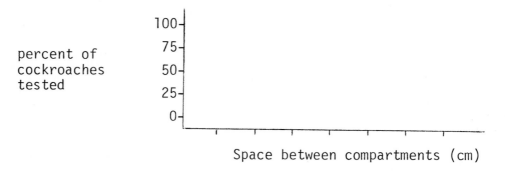

Space between compartments (cm)

===

NOTES:

  *(1) In the thigmotaxis experiment do you find that any class of
      cockroaches (males, females, nymphs) are consistently located
      above or below any other class of cockroaches?*

  *(2) Viewing will be easier if you use a Plexiglas box in the
      vertical-horizontal preference tests. In addition to recording
      vertical-horizontal preferences, check to see if the cockroaches
      are on open surfaces or in the cracks (thigmotaxis?).*

The cockroach now relates its intended direction of movement to the observer by the direction of movement of the sphere. Equispaced dots (of phosphorescent paint) enhance the ability of the observer in recording the direction of locomotion in the dark (if visual cues are to be eliminated). A styrofoam ball can also be carved into a continuous y-maze as shown in Fig. 6.11. This apparatus forces the cockroach to turn left or right at each junction.

Experiments with a fixed cockroach are basically the same as those with an arena   Orientation responses can be measured by recording the direction that the styrofoam ball or y-maze turns.

MATERIALS

Camera system (SLR or video)
1/8" dowels
Scotch spraymount adhesive
Styrofoam balls (5 to 10 cm diameter)
White glue
Phosphorescent paint (glows in the dark) or blacklight-reflecting paint

Ring stand and clamps
Bees wax or sealing wax
Odorants (female sex pheromone, optional)
Black and white cardboard
Petri dishes (optional)
Black plastic model paint
White light, red light or black light bulb and lamp
Sandpaper, razor knife

NOTES TO INSTRUCTOR

1. Most any robust walking insect can be used in the orientation experiments described in this chapter.
2. As cockroaches are negatively phototactic, the experiments with light have the highest success quotient.
3. The unique aspect of the fixed cockroach preparation is that students can view the walking and antennal movements up close. Note that when an insect is positioned upside-down with the weight of the styrofoam sphere pressing downward, this mimics norma! 'rightside-up' walking; when the sphere is 'held' below a cockroach, this mimics 'upside-down' walking.

GENERAL READINGS

Bell, W. J. 1981. Pheromones and Behavior. In: The American Cockroach, Ed. by W. J. Bell and K. G. Adiyodi. London: Chapman & Hall.
Camhi, J. M. 1980. The escape system of the cockroach. Sci. Amer. (Dec) pp. 158-172.
Fraenkel, G. S. and D. L. Gunn. 1961. The Orientation of Animals. New York: Dover (paperback).
Jander, R. 1975. Ecological aspects of spatial orientation. Annu. Rev. Ecol. Syst. 6: 171-182.

RESEARCH REPORTS

Bell, W. J. and T. Tobin. 1981. Orientation to sex pheromone in the American cockroach: analysis of chemotactic mechanisms. J. Insect Physiol. (in press).

Camhi, J. M. and W. Tom. 1978. The escape behavior of the cockroach *Periplaneta americana*. I. Turning response to wind puffs. *J. comp. Physiol*. 128: 193-201.

Camhi, J. M., Tom, W. and W. Volman. 1978. The escape behavior of the cockroach *Periplaneta americana*. II. Detection of natural predators by air displacement. *J. comp. Physiol*. 128: 203-212.

Roeder, K. D. 1959. A physiological approach to the relation between prey and predator. *Smithson. Misc. Collect*. 137: 287-306.

Rust, M. K., Burk, T. and Bell, W. J. 1976. Pheromone-stimulated locomotory and orientation responses in the American cockroach. *Anim. Behav*. 24:52-67.

Exercise—6.6—AGGRESSION: SEQUENTIAL BEHAVIORAL ACTS

Animals fight members of their own species for a variety of reasons. Competition for a mate, food, water, or suitable shelter may lead to fighting interactions. Some animals may fight to the death, but because of the high risk involved to both parties in such combat fighting, the behavior is often ritualized so that a winner may be determined without risk of injury to the parties involved. Dominant-subordinate relationships, where one animal displays a submissive posture to inhibit further attack by the other individual are found throughout the animal kingdom and occur in many species of cockroaches. Hierarchies, such as the peck-order found in some birds, are also present in some species of cockroaches.

Cockroaches make an ideal model system for studying aggression because it is easier to manipulate colonies of cockroaches than herds or packs of large mammals or flocks of birds in the laboratory, and because cockroaches display many of the same aggression-related phenomena as other species.

Three major areas of study are suggested: the role of aggression in determining the priority of individuals having access to resources; dominance behavior among individuals, leading to hierarchy formation; and sex differences as they relate to the previous two topics. The discussion below introduces some of the techniques used for these types of studies.

A. METHODS FOR OBSERVING AGGRESSION IN COCKROACHES. Most cockroaches exhibit aggression during the dark portion of the photocycle, in keeping with their nocturnal habits. To observe aggressive interactions it is best to use animals that have been habituated to a reversed light cycle for three to four days and to schedule the observations during the earlier portion (hours 2-6) of the dark part of the cycle. Nearly all of the species studied so far by researchers have aggressive behavior; it is easily elicited in Periplaneta americana, Nauphoeta cinerea, Gromphadorhina, Blaberus and Eublaberus. Aggression has also been observed in Blattella germanica but it does not occur in such high levels in this species.

B. AGGRESSIVE ACTS. How do we know when a cockroach is fighting? To understand aggression in any animal species it is necessary to supply a seemingly appropriate context. Unfortunately we apply values and opinions of human origin—we are anthropomorphic. Certain contexts are known to stimulate aggression in nearly all animals, however, and we will use these key situations to stimulate behavioral interactions that have a high probability of including aggression. These are (1) interactions between individuals that have not previously met, (2) starved individuals when provided with food, and (3) isolated males when provided with a virgin female. With some imagination you can instigate these and other aggression-stimulating contexts.

As cockroaches exhibit fighting, record the acts and attempt to define them. For example, kicking is a thrust of one of the legs against an opponent. Now you can record kicking each time it occurs. Fig. 6.12 shows a record of two hypothetical male animals fighting; the same methods shown in the figure can be used for two cockroaches. Are any of the aggressive acts also observed in courtship (Exercise 6.4)?

123

Data recording sheet:

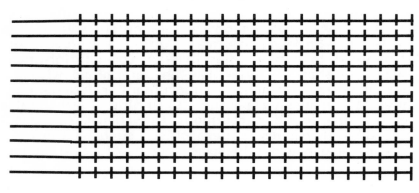

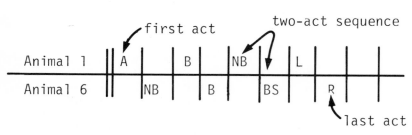

first act

two-act sequence

Animal 1   A   B   NB   L

Animal 6   NB   B   BS   R

last act

<u>Behavioral acts:</u>

A - approach   BS - back step
B - butt   L - lunge
NB - neck bend   R - retreat

Fig. 6.12. Transcription techniques for recording sequential behavioral acts in agonistic behavior of a hypothetical animal. Slots are available on the data sheets for recording sequences of acts of animal A (above the line) and animal B (below the line). To capture all of the behavioral details, dictate your behavioral observations on a tape recorder, and then transcribe these observations onto data sheets as shown in the figure.

C. MALE AGGRESSION: SOME VARIABLES. Usually males are more aggressive than females, although in Parcoblatta the reverse may be true. Groups of males kept in cages with 20-50 cm^2 floor space per individual (depending on the body size of the species employed) exhibit aggression among individuals in the group. Various environmental perturbations (e.g. shaking the cage, flashing a bright light at the animals), exposing them to female odor (sex pheromone), starvation, crowding, or introducing a new individual into the group will increase or decrease the frequency of aggressive acts observed.

D. IDEAS ON DATA ANALYSIS. One approach for testing the effect of treatments on aggression is to record the number of aggressive encounters between animals during a given time period. These encounters can also be divided into five levels of intensity, following the approach of Bell and Sams (1973); level one encounters occur when one animal approaches another one and one sided or mutual antennation occurs; level two encounters are characterized by rapid jerks of the body by one or both of the animals or by 'stilt-walking' where an animal raises itself off the substratum so it is taller than the opponent; level three encounters involve biting and/or kicking by one animal; level four encounters involve mutual biting and kicking; and level five encounters have intensive grappling. This scale is one of increasing intensity of fighting, and if each encounter observed is characterized by the highest level that it reachs, then the frequency of encounters at each level can be compared for treatment and control groups.

It is often possible to determine a 'winner' and 'loser' in an encounter. If animals are marked by painting or gluing numbers on their dorsum (Box #4), data can be collected to test for dominance hierarchies by keeping track of the individuals that each animal can defeat (Fig. 6.13). Does a 'winner' of one bout always win its fights? Can you characterize the behavior of cockroaches that win a high percentage of fights?

Since behavior is often quite variable, replicates are usually necessary to demonstrate differences between control and treatment groups. If five animals are used in a cage and each cage is observed for an hour, then five replicates for control and treatment are usually sufficient. Depending on the statistical approach used it may be easier to watch until a certain number of encounters have taken place, instead of using a fixed time period.

E. STATISTICAL ANALYSIS.

(1) Diversity of acts. Do male cockroaches use one act of aggression as commonly as all others? To test this hypothesis, count the total number of acts (N) recorded during your experiments and divide that number by the number of different acts (e.g. kicking, biting, etc) (A). The value obtained (e) is the number of times each act should occur, given that each act has an equal probability of occurring. Now run Chi-square tests using e as the expected and 0 as the observed values, and record these values in DATA BLANK II.

Example: In a system of 3 acts, the frequencies were kick (20), bite (100), lunge (66). N = 20+100+66 = 186; A = 3; e = 186/3 = 62.

$$\bar{x}^2 = \Sigma \frac{(0-e)^2}{e}$$

	A	B	C	D	E
A		0	1	0	5
B	6		5	11	12
C	10	18		12	10
D	10	3	4		12
E	1	0	0	0	

	C	B	D	A	E	W
C		18	12	10	10	50
B	5		11	6	12	44
D	4	3		10	12	29
A	1	0	0		5	6
E	0	0	0	1		1
L	10	21	32	27	39	

Fig. 6.13. Dominance hierarchies. Animals A,B,C,D, and E were paired with each other and a winner was determined for each bout, as shown in the left matrix. For example, of 11 bouts between A and C, A won 1 and C won 10. Then, by analyzing winner and loss ratios, the right matrix was constructed, attempting to put winners above losers. Note that no animal won a greater percentage of bouts from any animal placed above it in the matrix. W-wins, L-loses.

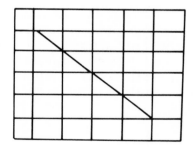

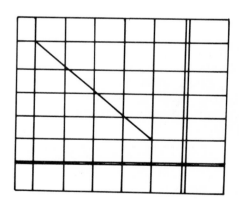

DATA BLANK I. Matrices for data on hierarchies (as above)

$$\bar{x}^2 = \frac{(20-62)^2}{62} + \frac{(100-62)^2}{62} + \frac{(66-62)^2}{62} =$$

$$x^2 = 28.45 + 23.29 + .25 = 52$$

$$P < .005$$

(2) <u>Two-act sequences</u>. Aggressive acts are information for animals. How specific is the information? If one individual kicks, will the opponent also kick or does it usually answer with a bite? Chi-square can be used to test this kind of hypothesis. List the frequency of all acts immediately following kick and follow the above routine to see if the acts that follow kick are selected at random or if one or two acts are selected more frequently.

Example: After one individual kicks, the other individual follows with: bite (72), lunge (28) (frequencies shown in parentheses). N = 72+28 = 100, A = 2, e = 100/2 = 50.

$$\bar{x}^2 = \Sigma \frac{(O-e)^2}{e}$$

$$\bar{x}^2 = \frac{(72-50)^2}{50} + \frac{(28-50)^2}{50} =$$

$$\bar{x}^2 = 9.68 + 9.68 = 19.36$$

$$P < .005$$

Chi-square shows that bite occurs more frequently than lunge.

MATERIALS

Cockroaches (adult males, *Nauphoeta* is best)
Plastic cages or shoe boxes (16L x 25W x 16H cm)

Red lightbulb
Taperecorder (optional)

NOTES TO INSTRUCTOR

1. Experiments should be performed under far red light lamps (600-650 nm); some photo darkroom lamps are appropriate, as are filters that can be purchased from Kodak or Edmund Scientific). If red lighting is not possible, use dim incandescent lamps.
2. Field crickets, <u>Acheta</u>, can be substituted for cockroaches, or they can be used to compare with cockroaches.
3. Sometimes animals will not instigate bouts of aggression no matter what kinds of conditions are presented; patience is required.
4. Taperecorders can be used effectively if the machines are equipped for transcription; some microphones control the 'on-off' function, and work satisfactorily for transcription.

```
================================================================================
```

DATA BLANK II. Diversity of acts in aggressive behavior

Name of act	Number of times observed	o^*	e^{**}	$o - e$	$\dfrac{(o - e)^2}{e}$
1					
2					
3					
4					
5					
6					
7					
8					
9					
10					
11					
12					
TOTAL (A):____	TOTAL (N):___		SUM $\dfrac{(o - e)^2}{e}$:____		

* Number of times each act was observed, divided by N

** N divided by A (A equals number of different acts)

```
================================================================================
```

128

GENERAL READINGS

Bell, W. J. 1981. Pheromones and Behavior. In: The American Cockroach. Ed. by W. J. Bell and K. G. Adiyodi. London: Chapman & Hall.

Brown J. L. 1975. The Evolution of Behavior. New York: Norton Press.

RESEARCH REPORTS

Bell, W. J. and R. E. Gorton, Jr. 1978. Informational analysis of agonistic behavior and dominance hierarchy formation in a cockroach, Nauphoeta cinerea. Behavior 67: 217-235.

Bell, W. J. and G. R. Sams. 1973. Aggressiveness in the cockroach Periplaneta americana (Orthoptera-Blattidae). Behav. Biol. 9: 581-593.

Breed, M.D., Smith, S.K. and B. G. Gall. 1980. Systems of mate selection in a cockroach species with male dominance hierarchies. Anim. Behav. 28: 130-134.

Ewing, L. S. 1973. Territoriality and the influence of females on the spacing of males in the cockroach, Nauphoeta cinerea. Behaviour 45: 287-304.

Nelson, M. C. 1979. Sound production in the cockroach Gromphadorhina portentosa. The sound production apparatus. J. comp. Physiol. 132: 27-28.

Ritter, H. Jr. 1964. Defense of mate and mating chamber in a wood roach. Science 143: 1459-1460.

Simon, D. and Barth, R.H. 1977. Sexual behavior in the cockroach genera Periplaneta and Blatta. III. Aggression and sexual behavior. Z. Tierpsychol. 44:305-322.

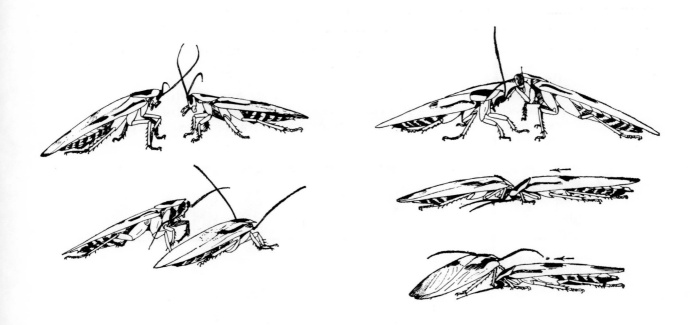

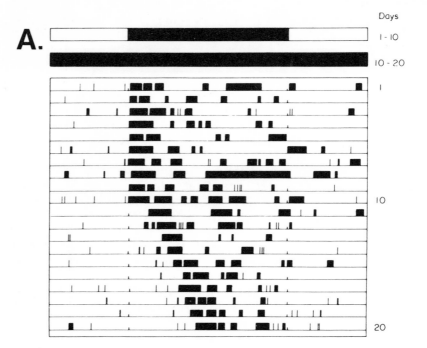

Fig. 6.14. (A) Locomotor activity of a cockroach, Leucophaea maderae, on a running wheel recorded by an actograph. Each horizontal line represents 24 hours; the vertical black bars indicate periods of activity. Successive days are arranged from top (day 1) to bottom (day 20). The animal was maintained for 10 days in a 12-hr light and 12-hr dark cycle. On day 11 the cycle was shifted to continuous darkness; activity continued to show periodicity, but began to drift away from solar time.

(B) Locomotor activity recorded by a photocell circuit across a cage of cockroaches, Periplaneta americana; two cages were tested simultaneously (upper and lower figures). The cycle is 12-hr light and 12-hr dark (shaded portion of figures). Notice that the cage represented in the lower diagram contained less active cockroaches than the upper cage.

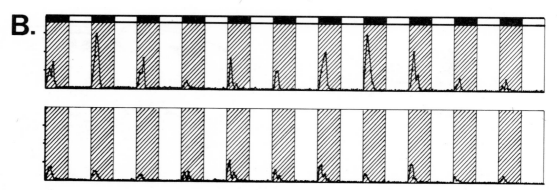

Exercise—6.7—ACTIVITY RHYTHMS: BIOLOGICAL CLOCKS

Most animals have endogenous rhythms of approximately 24-hour periods, so that certain behaviors or physiological events take place at about the same time in each 24-hour period. Cockroaches, for example, are active at night and inactive during the day. The questions explored in the following experiments are (1) what environmental cues set the rhythm, and (2) in the absence of these cues how long will the rhythm be exhibited?

A. ENVIRONMENTAL CUES. Using techniques described in the Methods Section, record activity of cockroaches in a 12:12 dark:light photocycle. When you have obtained these baseline data, the following changes can be made: 1) switch cockroaches so that it is now light in their active period and dark in their inactive period; 2) maintain animals in constant darkness or light (Fig. 6.14); 3) change from dark/light to noise/no noise or odor/no odor (can cues other than light set the activity rhythm?); 4) if the dark period is systematically reduced in length do cockroaches become more active during the light phase? Do these treatments alter activity rhythms? How do the results explain the factors controlling cockroach activity rhythms? Compare activity rhythms of cockroaches with those of other insects or small animals. Why is it that some animals are active at night, and others during the day?

B. PERCEPTION OF ENVIRONMENTAL CUES THAT 'SET' THE BIOLOGICAL CLOCK. With a fine brush, paint the compound eyes and/or the ocelli with opaque, black paint. Does either treatment alter the rhythm you have already recorded with unaltered cockroaches?

C. HOW DO COCKROACHES PARTITION THEIR TIME. What percent of their time is spent on the following activities: feeding, drinking, walking, antennal grooming, body cleaning, interacting with other cockroaches, doing nothing. How do these percentages compare with those of other animals, such as humans? Can you chart a typical cockroach day and night? Do activities during day 1 differ from those during day 2? If a portable tape recorder is available, recording your observations on tape will be helpful.

METHODS

Simplified activity monitors. Activity can be recorded in at least three different ways, from simple to complicated methods.

(1) Hand and eye. Plastic shoe boxes or mouse cages, each with greased sides and a transparent plastic top are required for this monitoring technique (Fig. 6.4). A black line is drawn across the bottom of each cage, connecting the two closest sides. When cockroaches are moving in the cage the number of times they cross the line in a given time period is recorded, providing a measure of activity (see Exercise 6.4). If the insects are not very active, add more lines to increase the sensitivity of the assay. Now, in order to alleviate the necessity of recording through a continuous 24-hour cycle, place 5 cages in a room with a 12:12 hour photocycle running the light phase at 8 p.m. to 8 a.m., and 5 other cages in another room running the light phase from 8 a.m. to 8 p.m. Thus portions of both dark and light phases are happening during normal

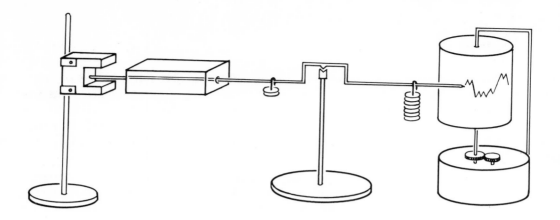

Fig. 6.15. Simple mechanical actograph. Cage at left holds cockroaches; their activity is translated to a pen on the moving drum.

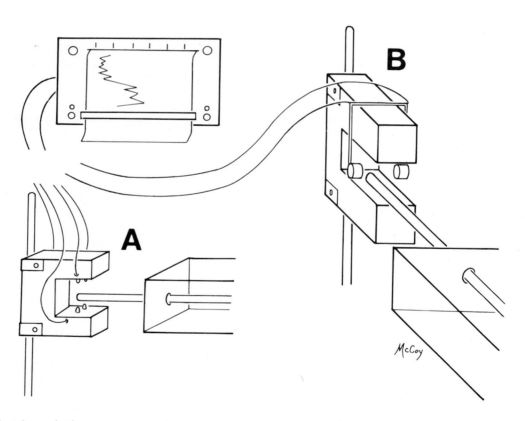

Fig. 6.16. (A) Same basic setup as in Fig. 6.15, but with an open switch in the restraining arm; when the metal bar contacts the switch, a chart recorder pen makes a line on the moving chart paper. (B) A photocell and light beam are used instead of an open circuit to activate a chart recorder pen.

'people' hours when measurements of activity can be made. If several darkrooms are available, of course, the recording times can be manipulated even more carefully, but more cages are required. Given that two light cycles are being used, observers should record the number of times cockroaches cross the line in one 5 minute period during each hour; the data are termed activity counts per minute when divided by the number of cockroaches in the cage (ACPM). The activity rhythms can be established by calculating the mean ACPM during each hour of the photocycle.

(2) <u>Mechanical methods</u>. An automatic activity recorder (actograph) can be constructed by linking together a horizontally moving piece of paper and a pen that moves vertically when the animal moves. The drum technique (Fig. 6.15) utilizes a cylinder on which a piece of paper can be attached; as the drum turns the pen writes on the paper. You can use a felt tip pen on regular paper or a wire against a piece of smoked paper. The drum must be turned by an old clock mechanism or an electric timing motor (from an appliance timer or purchased from an electronic supplier). There are many ways to make the pen move up and down on the paper; one example is shown in Fig. 6.15).

(3) <u>Electrical methods</u>. Activity can be 'sensed' by sound detectors, vibration detectors, light detectors and other such devices (Fig. 6.16). Usually these changes ultimately result in a change in the voltage output from the detector, and then an electronic event recorder moves a pen on chart paper in response to changes in voltage. Miller (1979) discusses electrical actographs in detail, and provides circuits for various types of instruments. Electronic books for beginners describe circuits for infra-red photocell detectors; these can be positioned across a cage of cockroaches, and will be actuated each time a cockroach interrupts the light beam focused on he photocell. Alternatively, the photocell and light beam can be positioned as shown in Fig. 6.16; this mechanism is similar to a burgler alarm across a doorway. Finally, instrument suppliers offer a variety of activity monitors that can be purchased and used immediately.

MATERIALS

Cockroaches: <u>Periplaneta</u> or <u>Leucophaea</u> recommended.
Plastic cages or shoe boxes
Red lightbulb and lamp
White lightbulb and lamp
Black magic marker
White paper

Electronic photocell circuit and event recorder (optional)
Portable tape recorder (optional)
Opaque black paint (varnish)

GENERAL READINGS

Beck, S. D. 1968. <u>Insect Photoperiodism</u>. New York: Academic Press.
Brady, J. 1974. The physiology of insect circadian rhythms. <u>Adv. Insect Physiol</u>. 10: 1-116.
Miller, T. A. 1979. <u>Insect Neurophysiological Techniques</u>. New York: Springer-Verlag.
Roberts, S. K. 1965. Significance of endocrines and central nervous system in circadian rhythms. In: <u>Circadian Clocks</u>, Ed. by J. Aschoff. Amsterdam: North-Holland.

Saunders, D. S.   1976.   The biological clock of insects.   <u>Sci</u>. <u>Amer</u>. (Feb)
pp. 114-121.

Sutherland, D. J.   1981.   Rhythms.   In: <u>The American Cockroach</u>, Ed. by
W. J. Bell and K. G. Adiyodi.   London: Chapman & Hall.

RESEARCH REPORTS

Rivault, C.   1976.   The role of the eyes and ocelli in the initiation of
circadian activity rhythms in cockroaches.   <u>Physiol</u>. <u>Entomol</u>. 1:
227-286.

Exercise-6.8—MAINTENANCE BEHAVIORS: FIXED OR FLEXIBLE?

Cockroaches exhibit behaviors that are sometimes categorized as 'fixed action patterns' or FAPs. FAPs are usually thought to be controlled internally and to be species-specific. Once initated they require few or no additional stimuli for their completion. The behaviors examined in this exercise illustrate fixed action patterns that are all involved in some way with the maintenance of the body.

A. <u>RIGHTING BEHAVIOR</u>. An animal commonly gets flipped onto its 'back,' and so the ability to turn over or to right itself is an extremely important behavior. The challenge is to determine how a cockroach performs righting behavior and to find out if the actions involved are identical each time the behavior is performed. Are the same legs involved in the same sequence every time you observe this behavior? If you remove one leg can righting still be performed using another leg?

B. <u>GROOMING</u>. To stimulate cockroaches to groom themselves when you are ready to observe them, smear a <u>light</u> coat of diluted honey and water on the body, legs and antennae. Record the sequence of grooming actions for as many replications as possible. Is the sequence fixed or is there some flexibility? Is there more variation among individuals than for one individual? If you cut off a leg, or an antenna does the cockroach still try to groom the missing appendage?

C. <u>TARSAL 'REFLEX.'</u> Tether a cockroach dorsally as described in Exercise 6.5. Now, pick up the cockroach by the tethering stick and notice the actions of the legs. Next, attach a string with wax to the pronotum and pick up the string. Why does the cockroach begin to flap its wings? Lastly, gently toss or drop a cockroach into the air (over an arena, to prevent escape), and see if it lands on its feet or its back. Do you obtain the same result if the wings are removed before beginning this experiment? How does a cockroach know what direction is up or down? Does an anesthetized cockroach perform as well as an awake individual?

D. <u>IMMOBILIZATION REFLEX</u>. Touch an adult Blaberid, such as <u>Blaberus</u>, <u>Byrsotria</u> or <u>Gromphadorhina</u>, on the pronotum. Usually the cockroach will stop moving and 'crouch' (Fig. 6.17). Try tactile stimuli with a wooden applicator stick, toothpick and a needle. Is the 'crouch' response directional, i.e. a touch on the right side of the pronotum elicits pressing of the body down on the right side? How far apart are the sensory cells positioned on pronotum?

MATERIALS

Adult cockroaches or other insects
  (large, slow moving preferred)
Honey (diluted with water)
Materials for tethering cockroaches
  (see Exercise 6.5)

Wooden applicator stick,
  toothpick needle
Wax
String
Tape recorder (optional)

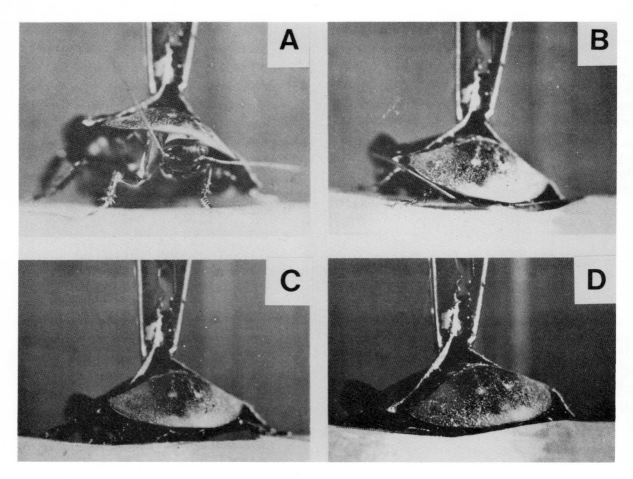

Fig. 6.17. Immobilization of <u>Blaberus craniifer</u> elicited by tactile stimulation of the pronotum. The clip attached dorsally maintains the cockroach in one place to facilitate close observation.

NOTES TO INSTRUCTOR

1. You may have to blow air on the cockroach suspended by a string to cause it to fly. Use a hairdryer turned to the 'cold' setting.
2. Only the slightest quantity of honey-water is needed to stimulate grooming in cockroaches, milkweed bugs, bees, and other insects.
3. Righting experiments should be performed on a rough surface, such as paper, to see normal executions; use a smooth surface such as glass to slow down the executions for making observations.

GENERAL READINGS

Carthy, J. D. 1971. An Introduction to the Behavior of Invertebrates. New York: Hafner Publishing Co.

Markl, H. 1974. Insect behavior: functions and mechanisms. In: The Physiology of Insecta, Vol. 3, Ed. by M. Rockstein. New York: Academic Press.

RESEARCH REPORTS

Kramer, K. and Markl, H. 1978. Flight-inhibition on ground contact in the American cockroach, Periplaneta americana. I. Contact receptors and a model for their central locations. J. Insect Physiol. 24: 577-585.

Reingold, S. C. and Camhi, J. M. 1978. Abdominal grooming in the cockroach: development of an adult behavior. J. Insect Physiol. 24: 101-110.

Zack, S. 1978. Description of the behavior of praying mantis with particular reference to grooming. Behav. Processes 3: 97-106.

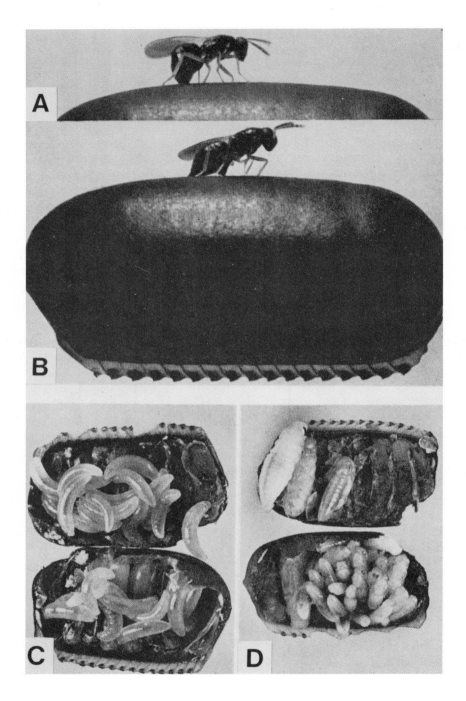

Fig. 6.18. Wasp parasite, <u>Tetrastichus hagenowii</u> (A-B) Female searching and laying eggs on an ootheca of <u>Periplaneta americana</u>, (C) larvae inside ootheca (feeding on cockroach embryos), (D) pupae inside ootheca.

Exercise—6.9—BEHAVIORAL ECOLOGY

The behavioral experiments described in this book mainly employ cockroaches that inhabit houses and other man-made structures. One can rationalize, therefore, that the arenas and boxes used in the experiments are fairly similar to natural environments encountered by cockroaches in our houses, and that the behaviors observed are not caused simply by the novelty of these environments. To understand cockroach behavior, however, you have to observe them in their natural habitats. Three such habitats are available for ecological investigations: man-made structures (cockroach-infested buildings), 'semi-natural' habitats such as woodpiles and natural habitats such as grasslands, forests, palmetto or deserts.

A. <u>LOCATING COCKROACH POPULATIONS</u>. Regardless of the habitat you choose to study (indoor or outdoor, natural or man-made), preliminary 'field work' is required to find suitable numbers of cockroaches to study. Remember that you will have to perform your study mainly in the evening and at night when cockroaches are most active. Some information, however, can be recorded during the day if you choose a problem such as the distribution of wood roaches in stacked firewood. There is only one way to locate cockroaches for ecological studies, and that is to get to work.

Monitoring cockroach populations can be accomplished actively or inactively. The active method means that you capture cockroaches with an insect net or with your hands. The inactive method involves trapping with jars set in the ground or in buildings; coat the inside of the jar with vaseline and bait with banana or bread-beer mixture. Of course, the active method is very time consuming. Using the trapping method you will gather more information per hour of work. But, can you list some of the potential bias in using food-baited traps?

A method of estimating population size is the 'capture-mark-release-recapture' of animals in samples of the population, over a period of time. Various techniques have been described to do this. The simpler methods include marking identically all captured animals. Since we cannot determine the time that these individuals were marked, only broad generalizations may be made from the results with regard to the dynamics of the population. For instance, if following several mark-recapture sessions the number of unmarked individuals is small, and we obtain a high recapture rate, it can be concluded that immigration into the population is low. Conversely, low recapture rates, and a high rate of new captures (unmarked) suggest that a high incidence of mixing of individuals is taking place within the population.

More sophisticated methods for estimating the total population size involve 'date-specific' and 'individual' marking. In the first method all of the animals captured at one time (session) are marked identically, but differently from animals marked in previous sessions and subsequent sessions (e.g., different colored labels). The most accurate (and most tedious) method is to mark each individual with a unique number or code when it is first captured. The results of even three mark-recapture sessions can provide important insights into the size of the population, as well as its demographic parameters, such as survival rate, mortality rate and birth rate. If you record the place where each marked individual was captured you can obtain information on dispersal rate, ranges of individual cockroaches, overlap between these ranges, sexes, age classes and species, and the affect of the distribution of food on the movement of cockroaches.

Manly and Parr (1968) described a simple, yet accurate, technique involving the 'date-specific' method. They take you through the marking, data formatting, analysis, and provide an example in such a way that you should be able to follow it using a cockroach population in a house, garage, wood pile, or wooded area. Remember, all mark-recapture methods, like other estimates, require that specific assumptions are met. Consult Southwood (1978) before deciding which method to use.

Taking complete notes is very important, because only from this information can your observations form a worthwhile study.

B. EXPERIMENTAL IDEAS FOR OUTDOOR STUDIES. By working outdoors you can attempt to answer the following questions:

(1) In what kinds of habitats are cockroaches found? What do they eat? Can you correlate any morphological adaptations of the digestive system to the types of foods they eat.

(2) What types of behaviors do cockroaches exhibit in logs, on trees, on the ground? At different parts of the night?

(3) In the sample of individuals you collect, what is the proportion of males, females and nymphs (sex ratio)? Are males found in different places than females? Do nymphs occur in the same places as adults? Do they feed on similar items?

(4) How does seasonality and changes in weather affect cockroach populations? (in terms of sex ratios, activity, preferred habitats).

(5) When are eggs laid? Nymphs hatched?

(6) What animals prey upon cockroaches? Are there any obvious physiological and/or behavioral strategies that cockroaches use to repell or escape from predators?

C. EXPERIMENTAL IDEAS FOR INDOOR STUDIES. By working in buildings infested with cockroaches, attempt to answer the following questions: (1) How many species inhabit the building? Do they occur together? Do they interact? (Some interesting lab experiments might be suggested).

(2) Where do cockroaches hide during the day? What is their activity cycle?

(3) Do cockroaches in buildings travel long distances and migrate from one space to another? Which stages in the life cycle migrate the longest distances?

(4) Can you observe cockroaches foraging for food, males searching for females (or vice versa), or females depositing egg cases?

(5) What animals prey upon cockroaches?

METHODS

Marking techniques. Refer to BOX #4.

Preparing a killing jar. Put 1" of sawdust in a jar and add ½" plaster of Paris. When the plaster dries, add about 5 ml. ethylacetate (which is available in some drugstores and from most chemical suppliers). When you go collecting, add 5 ml. of ethylacetate just before heading out.

MATERIALS

Labels or paints for marking
Jars for traps
Bait for traps
Notebook for outdoor recording

Clip board
Insect net
Dissecting microscope
Dissecting tools

GENERAL READINGS

Benton, A. H. and Werner, W. E. Jr. 1972. Manual of Field Biology and Ecology (5th ed.). Minneapolis: Burgess Publ. Co.

Oldroyd, H. 1958. Collecting, Preserving and Studying Insects. New York: MacMillan Co.

Peterson, A. M. 1959. Entomological Techniques (9th ed.) Ann Arbor, Mich.: Edwards Brothers, Inc.

Southwood, T.R.E. 1978. Ecological Methods, 2nd Edition. London: Chapman and Hall.

RESEARCH REPORTS

Berthold, R. and B. R. Wilson. 1967. Resting behavior of the German cockroach, Blattella germanica. Annals Entomol. Soc. Amer. 60: 347-351.

Edney, E. B. Haynes. S. and D. Gibo. 1974. Distribution and activity of the desert cockroach, Arenivaga investigata (Polyphagidae) in relation to microclimate. Ecology 55:420-427.

Bulow, F. J. and D. G. Huggins. 1968. Mark and recapture methods for studying domestic cockroach popultions. Iowa Acad. Sci. 75: 477-456.

Fleet, R. R. and G. W. Frankie. 1974. Habits of two household cockroaches in outdoor environments. Tex. Agric. Exp. St. Misc. Pub. 1153: 1-8.

Fleet, R. R., Piper, G. L. and G. W. Frankie. 1978. Studies on the population ecology of the smoky-brown cockroach Periplaneta fuliginosa in a Texas USA outdoor urban environment. Environ. Entomol. 7: 807-814.

Frishman, A. M. and I. E. Alcamo. 1977. Domestic cockroaches and human bacterial disease. Pest Control, June, P. 16.

Gautier, J. Y. 1974. Etude comparee de la distribution spatiale et emporelle des adultes de Blaberus atropos et Blaberus colosseus (Dictyopteres) dans quatre grottes de Trinidad. Rev. comp. Animal 9: 237-258.

Gorton, R. E. 1980. A comparative ecological study of the wood cockroaches in northeastern Kansas. Univ. Kansas Sci. Bull. 52: 21-30.

Gould, G. E. and H. O. Deay. 1940. The biology of six species of cockroaches which inhabit buildings. Purdue Univ. Agric. Exp. St. Bull. 451: 2-31.

Manly, B. F. J. and M. J. Parr. 1968. A new method of estimating population size, survivorship, and birth rate from capture-recapture data. Trans. Soc. Brit. Entom. 18: 81-89.

Piper, G. L. and G. W. Frankie. 1978. Integrated management of urban cockroach populations. In: Perspectives in Urban Entomology, Ed. by G. W. Frankie, and C. S. Koehler. New York: Academic Press.

Wharton, D. R. A., Lola, J. E. and M. L. Wharton. 1967. Population density, survival, growth, and development of the American cockroach. J. Insect Physiol. 13: 699-716.

Wharton, D. R. A., Lola, J. E. and M. L. Wharton. 1968. Growth factor and population density in the American cockroach, Periplaneta americana. J. Insect Physiol. 14: 637-653.

Appendix I STATISTICAL ANALYSIS

Statistics has been defined as the scientific study of numerical data based on natural phenomena. The science of applying statistical methods to the solution of biological problems is called biometry. Statistical analysis yields an objective evaluation of the results of an experiment or field observation. Statistics deals with quantities of information and not with a single piece of information. The data must be quantifiable to be analyzed. For example, measurements and counts can be analyzed statistically, but verbal descriptions cannot, unless they are numerically coded in some manner.

Some basic definitions are in order before we can continue. The data in a biometric study are generally based on individual observations or measurements taken on the smallest sampling unit. These smallest sampling units frequently, but not necessarily, are also individuals in the ordinary biological sense. If we measure weight in 100 rats, then the weight of each rat is an individual observation; the hundred rat weights together represent the sample of observations. However, if we had studied the weight in a single rat over a period of time, the sample of individual observations would be the weights recorded on one rat at successive times. The actual property measured by the individual observations is the character or variable. The sample observations are taken from a population. A population, in statistics, is defined as all of the observations that are made in a specific space and time about which inferences are to be made. A sample, then, is that part of the population that is actually measured. Most populations are too large to be measured completely. A representative sample is, therefore, used to draw conclusions about the entire population. This sample, however, must be random. That is, every individual in the population must have an equal chance of being selected.

Statistics give some indication of the validity of the differences seen in the results of a study. For example, if 10 out of 10 animals move toward a light source, one is fairly safe in saying that the species responds positively to light. But what if only 9 move toward the light, or 7 or 6? Is the movement in response to the light or is it merely random? Such data, taken from living systems, are affected by many (sometimes unidentifiable) causal factors, whose variation is uncontrollable. Statistical tests then give some indication of whether differences seen are true differences or whether they are merely random events.

A statistic is any quantity computed from raw data. Statistics tend to describe some general property of a data set, so that comparisons can be made with other data sets. Some of the more commonly used statistics and how they are calculated are give below:

1. Mean of the sample: $\bar{Y} = \dfrac{\Sigma Y}{n}$

   where $\bar{Y}$ = mean of the sample
   Y = an individual observation
   ΣY = sum of all the Y's
   n = sample size (number of observations)

2. Variance of the Sample (S^2):

$$S^2 = \frac{\Sigma Y^2 - \dfrac{(\Sigma Y)^2}{n-1}}{}$$

3. Standard deviation of the sample (S):

$$S = \sqrt{S_2}$$

To use statistics efficiently, the investigator must understand which statistical tests are most appropriate for each situation to be analyzed. Then experiments must be carefully designed to yield data in a form most amenable to the chosen analysis. The three analyses to be used in this laboratory are the t test, the X^2 test, and the Mann-Whitney U test. Each will be discussed separately.

A. t-test. This test can determine if a sample mean differs significantly from the population mean. (This difference could arise from some treatment applied to the sample.) The t statistic is determined as follows:

$$t = \frac{\bar{Y}_1 - \bar{Y}_2}{\dfrac{S_1^2 + S_2^2}{n}}$$

For this statistic, the degrees of freedom, df, = n-1.

To determine if the sample mean is significantly different from the mean of the entire population, determine the t statistic, above. Then decide on the level of significance (usually 0.05; results significant to this level would arise by chance alone 5% of the time). Find the value of the t statistic in the table for the degrees of freedom of the sample (df may be signified by 'μ' in the table). If the absolute value of the computed t statistic is greater than the t value in the table, your sample mean is different from the population mean at the 5% level of significance.

For example, suppose you have two sets of numbers from an experiment and you want to find out if the means are significantly different (n = 5 for each sample). Our hypothesis is that the means are equal.

Sample 1	Sample 2
9	5
7	3
6	1
5	2
8	4

$$\Sigma Y_1 = 35 \qquad \Sigma Y_2 = 15$$

$$\bar{Y}_1 = 7 \qquad \bar{Y}_2 = 3$$

$$\Sigma Y_1^2 = 255 \qquad \Sigma Y_2^2 = 55$$

First determine $\bar{Y}$, the mean for each sample. Then compute the variance.

$$S_1^2 = \frac{255 - \dfrac{(35)^2}{5}}{4} \qquad\qquad S_2^2 = \frac{55 - \dfrac{(15)^2}{5}}{4}$$

$$S_1^2 = \frac{255 - 245}{4} \qquad\qquad S_2^2 = \frac{55 - 45}{4}$$

$$S_1^2 = 2.5 \qquad\qquad S_1^2 = 2.5$$

144

Now plug these values into the t equation.

$$t_2 = \frac{7 - 3}{\dfrac{2.5 + 2.5}{5}} = \frac{4}{\dfrac{5}{5}} = \frac{4}{\sqrt{1}} = \frac{4}{1}$$

$$t_s = 4.00$$

Now look up the expected t value in the tables for df = 2(n-1) is 2(4) = 8, at α = .05. The table value is 2.306. Since the sample t_s is greater than the expected t, there is a significant difference between $\bar{Y}_1$ and $\bar{Y}_2$ at the 5% level. We reject our hypothesis that these means are equal.

B. <u>Chi-square test</u>. This test is more appropriate when biological variables are distributed into 2 or more classes (males/females; red/pink/white; in the light/in the dark; etc.). We can use the x^2 to test the goodness of fit of the observed frequency distribution to an expected frequency distribution based on some hypothesis. The x^2 statistic is calculated using this equation:

$$x_2 = \Sigma \frac{(\text{Observed} - \text{Expected})^2}{\text{Expected}} \qquad \text{for each class}$$

EXAMPLE: Flip a coin 100 times

Class	Observed (o)	Expected (e)	o-e	$(o-e)^2$	$\dfrac{(o-e)^2}{e}$
Heads	37	50	-13	169	3.38
Tails	63	50	+13	169	3.38
Total	100	100			$x^2 = 6.76$

In the example shown, x^2 = 6.76. The df = number of classes - 1; thus, df = 1. For an α of .05, the tabular critical value for the chi-square statistic is 3.84. Therefore, the distribution of heads and tails in this experiment differs significantly from that expected from the hypothesis that heads and tails come up at equal frequencies on a coin toss (50:50) and, thus, we reject this hypothesis.

C. <u>Mann-Whitney U test</u>. This test is probably the easiest of the three, although it looks formidable. This test compares two samples from a population to determine if they have the same distribution (and thus would not be significantly different). This test is performed as follows:

The data are first put in order and then graphed. One sample is selected (usually the one with the smaller number of observations), and for each observation in this sample, the number of observations in the other sample which are less in value are tabulated (ties count as ½). The total count is designated as C.

For example, suppose you have the following data for the wall-seeking behavior experiments:

W	NW	
55	50	
51	55	where: walled samples = n_1 = 6
62	48	
66	49	non-walled samples = n_2 = 6
49	52	
61	53	

145

These would be 'graphed' as follows:

W		49		51			55	61	62	66
NW	48	49	50		52	53	55			

Counting for W, $C = 1\frac{1}{2} + 3 + 5\frac{1}{2} + 6 + 6 + 6 = 28$ and $(n_1 n_2) - C = 37 - 28 = 8$.

U must be either C or $(n_1 n_2) - C$, whichever is larger. In this case C is larger, thus $u = C = 28$. Find u in the table.

From the table, the two samples are not significantly different at $= .05$, but they are significant at the 10% level (i.e., for $n_1 = 6$, $n_2 = 6$ at $\alpha = .10$).

The Mann-Whitney U test is a NONPARAMETRIC TEST, unlike the t test and chi-square tests. Thus you can use this test validly when your data (or experimental design) would make it invalid to apply a parametric test. Thus, this test is extremely valuable for studies such as behavioral experiments because it is quick, easy, and you don't have to worry about any underlying theoretical assumptions which must be met before a parametric test can be used.

GENERAL READINGS

Conover, W.J. 1971. Practical Nonparametric Statistics. New York: John Wiley & Sons.

Rohlf, F.J. and Sokal, R.R. 1969. Statistical Tables. San Francisco: W.H. Freeman and Co.

Sokal, R.R. and Rohlf, F.J. 1969. Biometry. San Francisco: W.H. Freeman and Co.

CRITICAL VALUES OF THE T-TEST

n	α			
	0.05	0.02	0.01	0.001
1	12.71	31.82	63.66	636.62
2	4.30	6.97	9.93	31.60
3	3.18	4.54	5.84	12.92
4	2.78	3.75	4.60	8.61
5	2.57	3.37	4.03	6.87
6	2.45	3.14	3.71	5.96
7	2.37	3.00	3.50	5.41
8	2.31	2.90	3.36	5.01
9	2.26	2.82	3.25	4.78
10	2.23	2.76	3.17	4.59
11	2.20	2.72	3.11	4.44
12	2.18	2.68	3.06	4.32
13	2.16	2.65	3.01	4.22
14	2.15	2.62	2.98	4.14
15	2.13	2.60	2.95	4.07
16	2.12	2.58	2.92	4.02
17	2.11	2.57	2.90	3.97
18	2.10	2.55	2.88	3.92
19	2.09	2.54	2.86	3.88
20	2.08	2.53	2.85	3.85
21	2.08	2.52	2.83	3.82
22	2.07	2.51	2.82	3.79
23	2.07	2.50	2.81	3.77
24	2.06	2.50	2.80	3.75
25	2.06	2.49	2.79	3.73
26	2.06	2.48	2.78	3.71
27	2.05	2.47	2.77	3.69
28	2.05	2.47	2.76	3.67
29	2.05	2.46	2.76	3.66
30	2.04	2.46	2.75	3.65
40	2.02	2.42	2.70	3.55
60	2.00	2.39	2.66	3.46
120	1.98	2.36	2.62	3.37
∞	1.96	2.33	2.58	3.29

CRITICAL VALUES OF THE CHI-SQUARE DISTRIBUTION

df	α				
	0.1	0.05	0.25	0.01	0.005
1	2.706	3.841	5.024	6.635	7.879
2	4.605	5.991	7.378	9.210	10.597
3	6.251	7.815	9.348	11.345	12.838
4	7.779	9.488	11.143	13.277	14.860
5	9.236	11.070	12.832	15.086	16.750
6	10.645	12.592	14.449	16.812	18.548
7	12.017	14.067	16.013	18.475	20.278
8	13.362	15.507	17.535	20.090	21.955
9	14.684	16.919	19.023	21.666	23.589
10	15.987	18.307	20.483	23.209	25.188
11	17.275	19.675	21.920	24.725	26.757
12	18.549	21.026	23.337	26.217	28.300
13	19.812	22.362	24.736	27.688	29.819
14	21.064	23.685	26.119	29.141	31.319
15	22.307	24.996	27.488	30.578	32.801

==

To use this table, compare your sample statistic $X^2 = \Sigma \frac{(O-E)^2}{E}$ with the value in the table with degrees of freedom equal to one less than the number of classes (df = n-1) when your hypothesis is external to your data, and at the chosen level of confidence. To obtain the 95% level of confidence, alpha must be 0.05. The null hypothesis that the observed and expected distributions are not significantly different is rejected when the sample statistic is greater than the tabled value. The alternate hypothesis states that the observed distribution is different in one direction than the expected.

CRITICAL VALUES OF THE MANN-WHITNEY STATISTIC

				α			
n_1	n_2	0.10	0.05	0.025	0.01	0.005	0.001
3	2	6					
	3	8	9				
4	2	8					
	3	11	12				
	4	13	15	16			
5	2	9	10				
	3	13	14	15			
	4	16	18	19	20		
	5	20	21	23	24	25	
6	2	11	12				
	3	15	16	17			
	4	19	21	22	23	24	
	5	23	25	27	28	29	
	6	27	29	31	33	34	
7	2	13	14				
	3	17	19	20	21		
	4	22	24	25	27	28	
	5	27	29	30	32	34	
	6	31	34	36	38	39	42
	7	36	38	41	43	45	48
8	2	14	15	16			
	3	19	21	22	24		
	4	25	27	28	30	31	
	5	30	32	34	36	38	40
	6	35	38	40	42	44	47
	7	40	43	46	49	50	54
	8	45	49	51	55	57	60
9	1	9					
	2	16	17	18			
	3	22	23	25	26	27	
	4	27	30	32	33	35	
	5	33	36	38	40	42	44
	6	39	42	44	47	49	52
	7	45	48	51	54	56	60
	8	50	54	57	61	63	67
	9	56	60	64	67	70	74

==

To use this table, compare your sample statistic to the above values in this manner:

1. Locate your sample sizes in the left two columns.

n_1	n_2	0.10	0.05	0.025	0.01	0.005	0.001
10	1	10					
	2	17	19	20			
	3	24	26	27	29	30	
	4	30	33	35	37	38	40
	5	37	39	42	44	46	49
	6	43	46	49	52	54	57
	7	46	53	56	59	61	65
	8	56	60	63	67	69	74
	9	62	66	70	74	77	82
	10	68	73	77	81	84	90
11	1	11					
	2	19	21	22			
	3	26	28	30	32	33	
	4	33	36	38	40	42	44
	5	40	43	46	48	50	53
	6	47	50	53	57	59	62
	7	54	58	61	65	67	71
	8	61	65	69	73	75	80
	9	68	72	76	81	83	89
	10	74	79	84	88	92	98
	11	81	87	91	96	100	106
12	1	12					
	2	20	22	23			
	3	28	31	32	34	35	
	4	36	39	41	42	45	48
	5	43	47	49	52	54	58
	6	51	55	58	61	63	68
	7	58	63	66	70	72	77
	8	66	70	74	79	81	87
	9	73	78	82	87	90	96
	10	81	86	91	96	99	106
	11	88	94	99	104	108	115
	12	95	102	107	113	117	124

===

2. Read down from your selected value of alpha. If you have chosen the 95% level of confidence, alpha is 0.05 (one-tailed test).

3. Find the indicated critical value of the statistic.

4. If your sample statistic is greater than the tabled value, the null hypothesis is rejected at the indicated level of confidence. The null hypothesis is that the two samples are not different (A = B). The alternate hypothesis states that one sample is more than the other.(A > B or B > A).

Appendix II SUPPLIERS OF ANIMALS, MATERIALS AND EQUIPMENT

A. <u>Cockroach</u> <u>suppliers</u>[1]:

Bioserv Ltd
38-42 Station Rd
Worthing, Sussex, England

Carolina Biological Supply Co.
Burlington, N. Carolina USA 27215

Connecticut Valley Biological Supply Co.
Valley Road
Southampton, MASS USA 01073

Griffin & George Ltd
Gerrard Biological Centre
Worthing Rd, East Preston,
West Sussex, BN16 1AS England

B. <u>Suppliers</u> <u>of</u> <u>materials</u>:

A.D. Mackay Inc.
198 Broadway
New York, NY USA 10038
(electrode wire)

Arnold R. Horwell, Ltd.
Laboratory & Clinical Supplies
2 Grangeway Kilburn High Road
London, NW6 1YB
England
(forceps, supplies)

Biolab Ltd.
2-10 Regent Street
Cambridge CD2 1DB
England
(supplies, labware)

BioQuip Products
P.O. Box 61
Santa Monica, Calif. USA 90406
(pins, nets, vials, mounting boxes)

Calbiochem-Behring Corp.
P.O. Box 12087
San Diego, Calif. USA 92112
(juvenile hormone, chemicals)

CENCO
Central Scientific Co. of California
6446 Telegraph Rd.
Los Angeles, Calif. USA 90022
(Tackiwax, other materials)

Clark Electromedical Instrumentation
P.O. Box 8
Pangbourne
Reading RG8 7HU
England
(electronic equipment and supplies)

Circon Microsurgical
Circon Corp.
749 Ward Drive
Santa Barbara, Calif. USA 93111
(watchmaker's forceps)

DIGI-KEY
Highway 32 South
P.O. Box 677
Thief River Falls, MN USA 56701
(electronic supplies)

Edmund Scientific
403 Edscorp Building
Barrington, NJ USA 08007
(electronic supplies; optics; motors)

ETCO Electronics
North Country Shopping Center
Rt. 9 North
Plattsburgh, NY USA 12901
(electronic supplies)

Fisher Scientific Co.
Zeltweg 67
8032 Zurich
Switzerland
(supplies)

Glasfabrik
Postfach 9
Malsfeld 3509
W. Germany
(electrodes)

Medwire Corp.
121 South Columbus Avenue
Mt. Vernon, NY USA 10553
(electrode wire)

Sargent-Welch
9520 Midwest Avenue
Garfield Heights
Cleveland, OH   USA   44125
(animal cages; 13x29x19 cm,
polystyrene, disposable)·

Sigma   Chemical Co.
P.O. Box 14508
St. Louis, MO   USA   63178
(juvenile hormone, chemicals)

C.   Suppliers of equipment:

Allco, Société D'instrumentation
   électronique
Allard et Compagnie
57, Rue Saint Sauveur
91160 Ballainvilliers B.P. 31
Longjumeau 91
France
(electronic equipment)

C.F. Palmer, Ltd.
Lane End Road
Wycombe, Bucks
England
(equipment)

Dorsch Elektronik
München 8
Worthstr. 8
W. Germany
(electronic equipment)

Electronics for Life Sciences, Inc.
P.O. Box 697
Rockville, MD   USA   20851
(electronic equipment)

Frederick Haer & Co.
P.O. Box 337
Industry Drive
Brunswick, ME   USA   04011
(electronic equipment; electrodes)

Grass Instrument Co.
101 Old Colony Avenue
Quincy, MASS   USA   02169
(electronic equipment; amplifiers)

Narishige Scientific Instruments
1754-6 Karasuyama-Cho
Setagaya-Ku
Tokyo
(electronic equipment, manipulators,
electrode pullers)

Scientific & Research Instrumentation, Ltd.
335 Whitehorse Rd.
Croydon, Surrey
England
(electronic and other equipment)

Shintron Co.
144 Rogers Street
Cambridge, MASS   USA   02142
(amplifiers, electrodes)

Tektronix, Inc.
P.O. Box 500
Beaverton, OR   USA   97005
(electronic equipment)

---

[1]The author will provide further information upon request about where to
obtain cockroaches anywhere in the world.

Appendix III   JOURNAL ABBREVIATIONS SPELLED OUT

Adv. Insect Physiol. - Advances in Insect Physiology

Amer. Midl. Nat. - American Midland Naturalist

Amer. Zool. - American Zoologist

Anim. Behav. - Animal Behavior

Anim. Learn. Behav. - Animal Learning and Behavior

Annals Entomol. Sci. Amer. - Annals of the Entomological Society of America

Annals Soc. Entomol. France - Annals of the Societé Entomologie de France

Annu. Rev. Ecol. Syst. - Annual Review of Ecology and Systematics

Annu. Rev. Entomol. - Annual Review of Entomology

Annu. Rev. Physiol. - Annual Review of Physiology

Appl. Ent. Zool. - Appled Entomology and Zoology

Behav. Biol. - Behavioral Biology

Behav. Processes - Behavioral Processes

Biol. Bull. - Biological Bulletin (Woods Hole)

J. Cell Biol. - Journal of Cell Biology

J. Chem. Ecol. - Journal of Chemical Ecology

J. comp. Physiol. - Journal of Comparative Physiology

J. Embryol. Exp. Morphol. - Journal of Embryology and Experimental
    Morphology

J. exp. Biol. - Journal of Experimental Biology

J. exp. Zool. - Journal of Experimental Zoology

J. gen. Physiol. - Journal of General Physiology

J. Kans. Entomol. Soc. - Journal of the Kansas Entomological Society

J. Insect Physiol. - Journal of Insect Physiology

J. Ultrast. Res. - Journal of Ultrastructural Research

Physiol. & Behav. - Physiology and Behavior

Physiol. Entomol. - Physiological Entomology

Proc. R. Soc. Lond. - Proceedings of the Royal Society of London

Quart. Micr. Sci. - Quarterly Journal of Microscopical Science

Res. Methods Instrument. - Research Methods and Instrumentation

Riv. Parasitol. - Rivista di Parasitologia

Sci. Amer. - Scientific American

Smithson. Misc. Collect. - Smithsonian Miscellaneous Collections

Symp. R. Ent. Soc. - Symposium of the Royal Entomological Society

Tiss. & Cell - Tissue and Cell

Univ. Calif. Publ. Entomol. - University of California Publications in
    Entomology

z. Tierpsychol. - Zeitschrift für Tierpsychologie

Appendix IV RELATIVE DIFFICULTY RATINGS OF EXPERIMENTS

Exercise designation	Rating*	Comments**
3 (Observing)	0.5	
4.1 (External anatomy)	2.5	2
4.2 (Internal anatomy)	3.5	2
5.1A (Feeding)	2.5	
5.1B (Digestion)	5.5(3.5)	2,4
5.1C,D (Diet)	3.5	2,1
5.2A,BC (Circulation)	5.0(4.0)	2,4
5.2D (Heartrate)	6.5(4.5)	2,4
5.3A (Ventilation)	5.0(3.0)	2,4
5.3B (Respiration)	7.0	2,3,5
5.4A (Reproductive cycles)	6.0	1
5.4B (Reproduction control)	8.0	1,2,3
5.4C (Ovulation)	3.0	2
5.4D (Parthenogenesis)	1.0	
5.5A-C (Embryos)	9.0	1,2,3
5.5C (4)(5) (Hatching)	1.0	
5.6A,B,D (Regeneration)	1.0	1
5.6C,E,F,G (Regeneration)	9.5	1,2,3
5.7A (Growth)	3.0	1
5.7B (Hormones)	6.0	1,2
5.7C (Tanning)	4.0	2
5.8A (Sense organs)	1.0	
5.8B (Electrophysiology)	9.5	2,3,5
5.9A,B,D (Locomotion)	5.0	1,2
5.9C,E (Locomotion)	2.5	
6.1 (Exploratory)	1.0	
6.2 (Learning)	4.5(1.5)	4
6.3A (Aggregation)	1.0	
6.3B (Pheromones)	7.0	1,2
6.3C-E (Pheromones)	5.0	
6.4 (Sex pheromones)	6.0	1,3
6.5 (Orientation)	7.5	1,2,3,5
6.5D,F (Orientation)	(2.5)	4
6.6 (Aggression)	6.0(4.0)	4
6.7 (Activity)	6.0	1,2,3
6.8 (Maintenance)	5.0(1.0)	4
6.9 (Ecology)	5.0(1.0)	1,3,4

---

*Rated from most difficult (10) to very simple (0)
**The following comments apply to some experiments:
1. Requires more than one lab period.
2. Manual dexterity skills needed.
3. Requires extreme patience.
4. Rating in parenthesis applies if statistical analysis and/or quantitative data collecting are omitted.
5. Non-standard laboratory instruments required for some experiments.

Appendix V GLOSSARY OF UNCOMMON TERMS

Aggression - fighting, initiating an attack.

Agonistic behavior - any behavior associated with conflict or fighting between two individuals, including escape or passivity.

Blaberid - belonging to the family Blaberidae (<u>Balberus</u>, <u>Leucophaea</u>).

Blattellid - belonging to the family Blattellidae (<u>Blattella</u>, <u>Supella</u>).

Blattid - belonging to the family Blattidae (<u>Periplaneta</u>, <u>Blatta</u>).

Cerci (singular: cercus) - small paired organs at the abdominal tip; found in males and females.

Chitin - polysaccharide material found in the cuticle.

Demography - statistical studies of populations with reference to density and capacity to expand or decline.

Distal - far from the point of origin.

Exoskeleton - another term for integument.

Frequency - the number of times that a periodic function (e.g. event) occurs in a certain length of time.

Ganglion (plural: ganglia) - a mass of nerve cells.

Gestation - period of embryonic development.

Haemocoel - body cavity.

Haemolymph - blood.

Integument - outer covering or arthropods; referring to the cuticle and epidermis, combined.

Model system - slang expression for a biological entity (population, organism, cell) with desirable attributes for study or experimentation.

Nota - plural of notum, as in pronotum.

Nymph - immature cockroaches; always wingless.

Olfactory - referring to odorous stimuli.

Oocyte - female germ cells within follicular tissue of the ovary.

Ootheca - cockroach egg case.

Oviposition - process by which eggs pass out of the oviduct through the genital chamber and out of the body.

Ovulation - process by which eggs pass out of the ovary and through the oviducts.

Parthenogenesis - reproduction in the absence of fertilization.

Preparation - an organism or part of an organism prepared in a certain way for experimentation.

Pronotum - largest dorsal thoracic tergite, partially shielding the head.

Proprioreceptors - sensory organs located within the body, usually involved in perceiving changes in muscle tone.

Proximal - near to the point of origin.

Releaser (of behavior) - specific sensory stimulus (or stimuli) that stimulates a particular type of behavior.

Respiration - physical and chemcial processes by which cells and tissues are supplied oxygen and relieved of carbon dioxide.

Ritualized behavior - communicative behavior that evolved from a noncommunicative behavior.

Roach - small, silvery freshwater fish (_Rutilus rutilus_); also, a term often used incorrectly to refer to cockroaches.

Saline - solution of salts equal in osmotic pressure to the blood of cockroaches.

Sclerotized - property of certain insect parts hardened and reinforced by an insoluble protein, sclerotin.

Shelter - any cardboard container or folded section of corrigated cardboard.

Sterna (singular: sternum) - ventral 'plates.'

Styles - small paired organs at the abdominal tip of males (and nymphs of some species).

Tactile - referring to mechanical stimuli, e.g. wind, touch.

Tanning - chemical process by which integument hardens and darkens in color.

Tarsus (plural: tarsi) - most distal leg segment.

Tegmina (singular: tegmen) - forewings.

Terga (singular: tergum) - dorsal 'plates.'

Tibia (plural: tibiae) - leg sigment between tarsus and femur.

Ventilation - process by which air is moved into and out of the body.

Sources of illustrations and other materials

Barth, R. H. 1970. The mating behavior of Periplaneta americana (Linnaeus) and Blatta orientalis Linnaeus (Blattaria, Balttinae), with notes on 3 additional species of Periplaneta and interspecification of female sex pheromones. Z. Tierpsychol. 27: 722-748. (Fig. 6.7; adapted from)

Bignell, D. E. 1981. Nutrition and digestion. In: The American Cockroach, Ed. by W. J. Bell and K. G. Adiyodi. London: Chapman & Hall. (Fig. 4.16; redrawn).

Camhi, J. M., Tom, W., and Volman, W. 1978. The escape behavior of the cockroach Periplaneta americana. II. Detection of natural predators by air displacement. J. comp. Physiol. 128: 203-212. (Fig. 6.8)

Camhi, J. M. 1980. The escape system of the cockroach. Sci. Amer. (Dec.) pp. 158-172. (drawing by Tom Prentiss) (Fig. 4.1)

Chen, D. H. 1968. Allatectomy of the American cockroach, Periplaneta americana (L.). In: Experiments in Physiology and Biochemistry, vol. 1, Ed by G. A. Kerkut, pp. 201-208. New York: Academic Press. (Fig. 5.1)

Cornwell, P. B. 1968. The Cockroach, vol. I. London: Hutchinson and Co. (Figs. 1.9, 1.10, 4.6 and keys for cockroaches)

Gautier, J.-Y. 1974. These, Docteur d'État, L'Université de Rennes. (Fig. 6.17 and sketches of cockroaches fighting).

Guthrie, D. M. and Tindall, A. R. 1968. The Biology of the Cockroach. London: Arnold Press. (Fig. 4.4)

Haber, V. R. 1926. The tracheal system of the German cockroach, Blattella germanica Linn. Bull. Brooklyn Entomol. Soc. 21:61-92. (Fig. 4.8)

Hughes, G. M. 1952. The co-ordination of insect movements. I. The walking movements of insects. J. exp. Biol. 29: 267-284; Modified by Chapman, R. F. 1969. The Insects, Structure and Function. New York: American Elsevier Publ. Co. (Fig. 5.15).

Lefauvre, J.-C. 1969. Thèse, Docteur és Sciences Naturelles, (Fig. 4.3).

Miall, L. C. and Denny, A. 1886. The Structure and Life-History of the Cockroach (Periplaneta orientalis), An Introduction to the Study of Insects. London: Lovell Reeve & Co. (Figs. 2.7, 4.9, 4.10, 4.13, 4.14, 4.15; redrawn, sometimes modified).

Oakley, B. and Schafer, R. 1978. Experimental Neurobiology, A Laboratory Manual. Ann. Arbor: University of Michigan Press. (Fig. 5.14; redrawn).

Roberts, S. K. 1962. Circadian activity rhythms in cockroaches. II. Entrainment and phase shifting. J. cell comp. Physiol. 55: 99-110; Modified by Matthews, R. W. and Matthews, J. R. 1978. Insect Behavior. New York: John Wiley & Sons. (Fig. 6.14A)

Roth, L. M. and Willis, E. R. 1954. The biology of the cockroach egg parasite, Tetrastichus hagenowii (Hymenoptera, Eulophidae). Trans. Amer. Entomol. Soc. 80:53-72 (Fig. 6.18).

Roth, L. M. and Willis, E. R. 1958. An analysis of oviparity and viviparity in the Blattidae. Trans. Amer. Entomol. Soc. 83:221-238. (Figs. 5.4, 5.9).

Roth, L. M. and Willis, E. R. 1960. Biotic associations of cockroaches. Smithson. Misc. Coll. 141:1-470. (Figs. 1.3, 1.4, 1.5, 1.6, 1.8)

Roth, L. M. and Stay, B. 1962. Oocyte development in Blattella germanica and Blattella vaga (Blattaria). Ann. Entomol. Soc. Amer. 55: 633-642. (Fig. 5.5; redrawn).

Seelinger, G. and Tobin, T. R. 1981. Sense organs. In: The American Cockroach, Ed. by W. J. Bell and K. G. Adiyodi. London: Chapman & Hall. (Figs. 4.2, 4.5).

Tanaka, A. 1976. Stages in the embryonic development of the German cockroach, Blattella germanica Linn. (Blattaria, Blattellidae). Kontyu 44: 512-525. (Fig. 5.7; Table I).

Welsh, J. H. and Smith, R. I. 1960. Laboratory exercises in Physiology. Minneapolis: Burgess Publ. Co. (Figs. 5.2, 5.3 and the section on Gas Mixtures)

INDEX